D1106965

# *ME AND BOGIE*

# ME
# AND
# BOGIE

*And Other Friends and Acquaintances
from a Life in Hollywood and Beyond*

*ARMAND DEUTSCH*

G. P. PUTNAM'S SONS
*New York*

G. P. Putnam's Sons
*Publishers Since 1838*
200 Madison Avenue
New York, NY 10016

Excerpt from *Field of Dreams* © by Universal Pictures,
a division of Universal City Studios, Inc., courtesy of MCA
Publishing Rights, a division of MCA, Inc.

Excerpt from *Bennett Cerf's Treasury of Atrocious Puns*
courtesy of Phyllis Cerf Wagner.

"Me and My One-Nighters with Sinatra" originally appeared
in *McCall's* in a slightly different form.

"Me and My Very Own Lemonade Stand," "Me and the Crime of the
Century," and "Me and My Double Life" originally appeared in *Chicago*
in a slightly different form.

Copyright © 1991 by Armand S. Deutsch
Introduction © 1991 by Sidney Sheldon
All rights reserved. This book, or parts thereof,
may not be reproduced in any form without permission.
Published simultaneously in Canada

Library of Congress Cataloging-in-Publication Data

Deutsch, Armand.
Me and Bogie: and other friends and acquaintances from a life
in Hollywood and beyond / Armand Deutsch.
p. cm.
ISBN 0-399-13595-2 (alk. paper)
1. Deutsch, Armand.   2. Motion picture producers and directors—
United States—Biography.   I. Title.
PN1998.3.D48A3  1991          90-24139 CIP
791.43'0232'092—dc20
[B]

Designed by MaryJane DiMassi
Printed in the United States of America
1   2   3   4   5   6   7   8   9   10

This book is printed on acid-free paper.

*My warm thanks to some good friends:*
*David Columbia, Perry Leff, Sidney Sheldon,*
*Ed Victor, and Michael Viner*

*For Harriet,*
*with all my love*

# CONTENTS

# INTRODUCTION

ARMAND DEUTSCH is not a name you will often come across in the daily newspapers or in the tabloids, although he is a name familiar to many celebrated and distinguished personalities over the past six decades. By birthright and by natural disposition, he has led a charmed life.

An extraordinarily engaging man with a warm wit and a writer's interest in people, Ardie, as he is known to his friends, was born the grandson of the great Chicago philanthropist Julius Rosenwald, founder of Sears, Roebuck & Company. When he was nine years old two rich young psychopaths named Loeb and Leopold, seeking the ultimate in perverted thrills, plotted to kidnap and murder the young scion. By a stroke of fate, their heinous plan befell another, becoming known as the crime of the century.

After college and a stint in the Navy, Ardie joined a Wall Street brokerage firm for which he quickly learned he had no interest. When a friend offered him the unlikely position as talent coordinator for the Rudy Vallee radio show, Ardie took it. Thus began his initiation into show business, which is amusingly recounted in this book's chapter "Me and the Barrymores."

During that period of his life, at a dinner party in New York, Ardie met Dore Schary, then the young head of production for RKO Studios. The two men became fast friends and much to Ardie's surprise, Schary invited him to go to Hollywood to become his assistant. Those were the halcyon days of the movie industry and Ardie didn't hesitate very long before accepting the offer. As luck would have it, Dore Schary not long after was recruited to head production at MGM. He took Ardie with him as a producer. That was where my friendship with him began. He was producing a movie called *Three Guys Named Mike,* starring Jane Wyman, Van Johnson, and Howard Keel. I wrote the screenplay. It was then that I too fell under Ardie's spell. He and his lovely wife, Harriet, and I have been friends ever since.

As he is quick to point out about himself, Ardie is a man who never set out to win friends and influence people. Much to his surprise and pleasure it just happened to him. Some have a talent for making connections. Ardie has a talent for making friends. *Me and Bogie* is a fascinating recollection of some of those friendships, told with Ardie's special insight, some of it into an earlier, gentler era. The reader is in for a great treat.

SIDNEY SHELDON

# ME

*and*

# MY FATHER

WHEN I WAS seven years old my father took me by train from our home in Chicago to South Bend, Indiana, to see the University of Notre Dame play Nebraska. I realized later that I was not his companion of choice. I was too young to grasp the thrill of seeing the brilliant Notre Dame backfield, already known as "The Four Horsemen," inch another step toward immortality on a beautiful fall afternoon under the Golden Dome of America's college football capital. We two were Indiana-bound because my mother, like so many mothers before her, had insisted that my father spend some quality time with me.

He did not want a ward. He wanted companionship and, as was his wont, he found it. He was not an alumnus of Notre Dame or Nebraska but had matriculated at Cornell. Although he was on campus for only six weeks before he was separated out from the college, his interest in Cornell football never diminished. By coincidence, which so often played into his hand, he met several other Cornellians. These worthies roamed the train, liberally toasting Cornell's hope for success that afternoon against their Ivy League opponent.

When the train pulled into the South Bend station he was not present. I was about to debark alone and uncertainly when he came tearing up. His attitude was that I had somehow gotten lost but that he forgave me.

Ensconced in our fifty-yard seats, which were his hallmark, he was a perfect role-model father. Unfortunately, on the return trip to Chicago he met up with his newfound friends and insisted on bringing them home. By the time we arrived at the house a great deal of liquor had been consumed. All my mother saw of the great day she had envisaged was her seven-year-old son together with four quite drunken men. She was understandably not overjoyed, though by this time she could not have been completely surprised. My father never did a mean thing. He was simply very young, very high-spirited, and had higher priorities than parental responsibility.

He showed his hand early by missing my arrival onto the planet. Conventional wisdom, of course, had it that he should have been on hand, sober and concerned, lending moral support to his wife. Such was not the case. He and his great crony, Ernest Byfield by name, were out on the town, prematurely celebrating my pending arrival. So seriously did they take this self-appointed task that it was many hours later before they entered the hospital, somewhat the worse for wear. They were shown immediately to the glass panel separating the viewers from the babies. I was pointed out to my father by a dutiful nurse. I was crying hard. This seemed unwarranted to Byfield, who said to my father, "What the hell does this boy have to cry about?" My father agreed and, for some inexplicable reason, failed to visit my mother before resuming his rounds.

Byfield was the owner of the famous Ambassador Hotels and, unlike my father, he worked hard. He was, however, a kindred spirit and all too often made time to join my father in pursuits that were invariably distasteful to my mother. He had one particular hobby revolting to her, and even to Byfield's strongest supporters. It was the law at that time in the State of Illinois that a condemned man be hanged by the neck until dead in the State Capital at Springfield. Witnesses were required. Occasionally, Byfield would volunteer for this grisly chore, packing a box lunch for the train trip. He sometimes prevailed on my father to accompany him. Although my father, unlike Byfield, did not enjoy executions, he was devoted to Byfield and not difficult to persuade when asked to assist in what Byfield referred to as "the business of the State."

My mother had been raised by protective, loving, financially privileged parents in a cotton batting of protection that would be impossible to duplicate today. Television news programs alone would have made that sort of upbringing impossible. There were, however, none of the constant intrusive battering that overload the mind of everyone, adult and child alike, in today's world.

She was brought up in a mansion on Ellis Avenue, a then fashionable South Side district of Chicago. Her father, Julius Rosenwald, was a titan of the day who built Sears, Roebuck into a huge company, acquiring a large fortune in the process. He was one of the country's leading philanthropists and an adviser to presidents. His wife, Augusta, was an active, functioning wife and mother, well known throughout Chicago for her civic activities. Day by day these two people lovingly went about the business of cloistering their daughter from the realities of that gentle era. They sent to the marriage altar an eighteen-year-old young woman whom they never would have permitted to travel alone on the deluxe 20th Century Limited from Chicago to New York. She was no more equipped to cope with her high-spirited, tippling bridegroom than to be an astronomer.

My father, in true Andy Hardy fashion, was brought up across the street. He was the son of an important executive of Inland Steel Corporation and lived not in a mansion but in a spacious, lovely home. To say that he wanted for nothing would be an understatement, although his future father-in-law's overriding success tended to diminish everyone around him. His early years were marked by the fact that his mother spent most of her adult life in mental institutions, coming home only infrequently for unsatisfactory visits and causing her husband to become increasingly reclusive. There was no real rudder to my father's formative years, and he certainly brought no maturity to this union. They were indeed two eggs not yet ready to make an omelet.

My mother was destined to become, some years later and remarried, an important, vital citizen of New York. When she died, in 1960, the speakers at the Memorial Service in her honor included Governor Nelson Rockefeller, Mayor Robert Wagner, and Mrs. Franklin Delano Roosevelt. She was a great ornament to the city, but she was a late bloomer.

Her major effort during her first marriage was to try to contain my father, who was an early bloomer. He was beautifully groomed and dressed, energetic and handsome. What set him apart was the simple fact that, in Carl Sandburg's city of "Hog butcher for the world," he did not work. He was Chicago's lone young idler. He might as well have worn a scarlet *I* on his forehead. What seemed to others a carefree, enviable life was in reality a lonely, uphill struggle. With better luck he would have lived in the South of France, where not working was commonplace and considered a virtue. In Chicago he was clearly the wrong man in the wrong place at the wrong time.

His sporadic efforts to enter the world of business were fitful and exotic. Once he came home and proudly announced that he had purchased at a bargain price a shop that rented costumes for fancy dress balls. He realized that such parties were not exactly the staple of Chicago entertaining, but he countered critics of his acquisition with his carefully thought-out business plan. He would launch his enterprise by hosting a lavish fancy dress ball and require all who were invited to outfit themselves at his shop. This, he reasoned, would certainly get it off to a booming start. His strategy did not work over the long term or even the short term, and the enterprise folded quickly.

Parties were his true metier and he was a much sought-after guest. His attractive looks and personality were only enhanced by his liberal libations. Without ever having had a lesson, he played the piano wonderfully. He loved Broadway show tunes and took the train to New York often enough to be thoroughly abreast. He had a habit of buying an extra theatre ticket for his overcoat, which drove my maternal grandfather, generous in charity matters but otherwise frugal, up the wall.

These train trips were colorful. He somehow acquired a small portable organ that, when folded, resembled a coffin for a pygmy. He took it with him on his travels. Organ music emanating from the open door of his stateroom was a great attention-getter, and his newfound friends were invariably invited to partake of his well-stocked liquor supply housed in a carefully packed suitcase.

Like many people with time on their hands, my father loved the movies and attended regularly. He was particularly partial to a popular short subject of the day called "The Fitzpatrick Travel Talks," which described in glamorous terms different places on the earth's surface. Mr. Fitzpatrick never thought of himself as a travel agent. His output was simply escapism to faraway places that, in those pre-airplane days, were as remote to motion picture audiences as a journey to the moon.

My father, however, was not the average moviegoer. Occasionally one of the Fitzpatrick offerings was irresistible to him. Off he would go virtually from the movie palace to India, absenting himself from home and fireside for many months.

I spent my earliest summers in a house on my grandfather's estate in Ravinia, a suburb of Chicago. Here my father's escapades took on an outdoor tone. Some were as gentle as a summer breeze; others more abrasive.

The property fronted on the blue, and then unpolluted, waters of Lake Michigan. Deeply wooded ravines interlaced with tanbark trails covered the areas between the houses. My father loved to run through these trails on beautiful moonlit nights, whooping and hollering in high spirits. It was a source of great embarrassment to my mother, especially since it was impossible to track him down. At a dinner party one night Ernie Byfield, ever helpful, gave my mother a cowbell which, if properly attached to him, he explained would simplify the problem of locating him. It would be hard to imagine a less well-received gift.

He loved fast, state-of-the-art motorcars and drove them around the area like Barney Oldfield. Speeding tickets were part and parcel of his daily rounds. A court reporter unearthed the fact that he had recently been arrested three times in one day by the same police officer. He did a job on my father's driving habits that was a worthy precursor of the investigative reporting technique that became a commonplace decades later.

Before the dust settled, the reporter learned and duly printed that my father had a vast cache of speeding summonses that had been ignored, that he had given gifts of cash to a great many traffic cops and had helped several with school tuition. To cap the climax, he had given one police officer a raccoon coat.

His court appearance, even in this quiet suburb, was covered by a sizable group of newsmen. He received a large fine and the temporary removal of his license. On its return he was required to put on his car a new device that held the speed to fifty miles an hour. He handled the matter with his usual aplomb, saying that he thought these speed regulators were an excellent idea and that he was proud to be one of the first to have one. All of this was bitter medicine to a father-in-law who was as publicity-shy as Garbo.

A specific example of my father at the wheel remains clear and verdant in my mind to this day. It was late in the afternoon on a warm Midwestern day. My mother had some guests to tea on the screened-in porch of our home. I happened to be there. We became aware of my father speeding down the long, curving, pebble driveway from the main road. He was at the wheel of his Stutz Bear Cat roadster with its giant hood and the handbrake outside the car. Our awareness increased by the second as it became apparent that the car was out of control. He came into sharp focus as he approached the picket fence fronting the lawn, desperately pulling at the brake. The car barreled through the fence, coming to rest within fifteen feet of wiping out the entire tea party.

He was at his best in these self-induced crises. He jumped out of the car in his tennis clothes with great energy, kissing my mother, greeting the guests profusely, telling them how nice it was to see them. Having created this frightening situation, he was in complete command of it, almost successfully conveying the impression that this was a normal manner of arriving home. Within two minutes he was on his way upstairs for his shower, leaving the guests staring at the Stutz Bear Cat just barely far enough away from them to postpone their demise.

By the end of my seventh grade, my mother had enough of his charming but highly unusual ways. Divorce proceedings, far more unusual than today, were started. My grandfather felt she would be happier living in Paris for a year, away from the press in new surroundings. I was told about the divorce so obliquely that it was quite a time before I grasped its full significance. I had a very real sense of loss, partially masked by the fact that I was embarking on a new life.

And so it was that I attended eighth grade in Paris. Only in retrospect did I realize how completely isolated I was from the French. I attended the American School, established for the

children of families who did not want their education interrupted by the language barrier. French was part of the curric-
ulum, but it was taught almost as though the school were
located in Chicago. I naturally spoke only English with my
classmates.

We did have a handsome Parisian butler whose secondary
assignment was to teach me French. I did not apply myself;
he did. At the end of the experience I spoke very little French.
He, on the other hand, spoke very passable English.

An American tutor took me everywhere. We did not miss
a museum, a park, or an arrondissement. He was methodical
and conscientious, but since he had no fire in his belly about
the city it was a plodding experience. My father would have
been the perfect guide to teach me the magic of Paris.

The high point of my year stands out in my mind as clearly
as the Eiffel Tower. We were at the Roland Garros Stadium
watching Bill Tilden and Bill Johnson playing Davis Cup dou-
bles against the French team of Henri Cochet and Jean Borotra,
when word spread like wildfire that an American was flying
the Atlantic Ocean solo. Along with all of Paris, we made our
way to Le Bourget Airport. I was there when Lindbergh
landed. In truth, I did not get so much as a glimpse of him
since the plane and the airport were small and the crowd was
vast. Oddly enough, that proximity remains a high point for
me.

I got to meet him a few days later in London, where Lindbergh went from Paris. My grandfather, who was in London,
arranged for me to cross the Channel and attend the Embassy
reception in his honor. It was a great thrill, but secondary to
the brilliant, clear night when I almost saw him land.

Before we departed Paris, my mother married a doctor, the
psychiatrist who had seen her through the rockier days of life
with my father. On our return to the United States we settled
in New York and they had a happy marriage which lasted the
rest of their lives.

My father, for reasons never known to me, had also moved
to New York and lived less than twenty blocks away from
me. He had a new bride who marked the beginning of a succes-
sion of short-lived marriages. Although he yielded parental

responsibility to my newly acquired stepfather, we two developed a warm friendship very meaningful indeed to me. He regularly took me to theatre, baseball games, and tony restaurants.

Only once did he venture into the field of parental advice. The subject was sex. The cornerstone of his emphatic viewpoint related to daughters of friends. Intimáte relationship with "these girls," as he branded them, were to be guarded against like the bubonic plague. The risk factor was limitless, including pregnancy and, God forbid, marriage. The young married women at the country club were a different kettle of fish. It was appropriate to pursue them. They had the twin virtues of being attractive and discreet.

His persona never changed. He was unfailingly casual, pleasant, and courteous. The best seats, the best tables, the fastest cars flowed his way naturally. His dependency on alcohol increased, but never to the point where it was off-putting.

In 1933 he went with a relatively new bride to Mexico. There he got caught in a fearful typhoid epidemic and died quickly. He could not have been enticed there by a Fitzpatrick Travel Talk; they had long since passed from the scene. I was in my sophomore year at Dartmouth when I heard the news. I was heartbroken. He was forty-one years of age. He would certainly have failed a litmus test on the qualities and virtues of a garden variety of father, but he brought into my life a sense of fun and adventure. The simplest things we did together had the gay mood of a successful party. His unique parental role could have been conceived and written by F. Scott Fitzgerald, and that's not all bad. How many people have a father like that?

He left me the sum of ten thousand dollars, together with a handwritten letter saying that during his lifetime he had gone through a considerable sum of money and had his present wife to support. He said with assurance that his tailor was the best in the business and urged me to spend my inheritance there, which I did. In those days the finest custom-made suit in New York cost less than three hundred dollars. Within two years I accumulated an awesome wardrobe.

He also left me a handsome pair of monogrammed cuff links

bearing his initials and mine. It is over half a century since his death and I wear them often. To this day I never put them on without a smile of remembrance, rather like tipping a hat. The smile is a bit wistful, since I am certain that he passed along to me some of the characteristics that did not serve him well.

# ME

*and*

# MY VERY OWN
# LEMONADE STAND

IN THE SUMMERS of my pre-camp years, from about 1913 to 1925, I lived with my parents and brother on a large family compound in Ravinia, which was noted then as now for its splendid music festival.

My grandparents' house, dominating the compound, was known to all of us as the Big House. And big it was, fronted by a magnificent expanse of lawn that would have made a testing par-five dogleg on any championship golf course.

The house was a mansion. Someone recently sent me a brochure extolling its size, grandeur, and dignity. It contained two large living rooms, a stately dining room and breakfast room, a glassed-in sun porch, and, below, a handsome billiard room. On the second floor were my grandparents' suite, a library/music room, and endless bedrooms. The third floor held a stately ballroom and innumerable rooms for servants.

One of those second-floor bedrooms was "mine," and I slept over regularly. In many ways, this house was a hub of my life—as was my grandfather himself. Although he cut a giant swath in Chicago and way beyond it, I knew nothing of his wealth and fame until considerably later. I realize in retrospect that considerable skill and effort went into normalizing my role as the oldest grandson of Julius Rosenwald. Such was his nature, and he imbued his family with it.

The houses of other family members were scattered helter-skelter, and the large area in front of our homes faced Sheridan Road. Although it was one of the main roads winding north from Chicago, no one ever dreamed of using the protective high fences and alarm systems that today are considered to be so basic and vital. All entrances were wide open, and to my knowledge no one except invited guests ever intruded.

My cousins, my brother, and I lived a rather reclusive life. There was a marvelous playground replete with swings, teeter-totters, slides, parallel bars, and benches that overlooked a large cutting garden. By general agreement the garden was out of bounds.

My great joy was our daily visit to the country club for tennis lessons. I loved both tennis and the club. My friends spent much time there, but family policy severely restricted our excursions, both as to time and to expenditures for such vital items as tennis balls and chocolate sodas. My grandfather was strict about such matters—and in those simple, uncomplicated days such decisions were not questioned.

Other children came to visit us, of course. And there were always the formalized "nature lessons," most of which were held at our house. They were presided over by a Mrs. Colton, a small, middle-aged, twittery woman whose specialty was birds.

Plump, stuffed specimens skillfully mounted on artificial tree branches were used as models, and Mrs. Colton, in a truly magical way, would make them appear as if from nowhere. As fast as her arm permitted, she would whisk bird and branch through the air with a flying motion while whistling the appropriate bird call, and then they would disappear again. Our object was to provide instant recognition, and our total and steady failure never got her down. We disliked her, but we saved our heartiest loathing for one another and for the class itself. For reasons unknown to me, we rarely went outdoors, although the compound was filled with innumerable birds, butterflies, and flowers.

One afternoon during such a class, my father appeared in our entryway, a bit worse for wear following several post-tennis drinks at the club. He looked in at us momentarily and would have proceeded without interrupting the lessons except for the cheery Mrs. Colton, who asked him if he would care to tell us his favorite flower. "The bastard toad flax," he replied, and went upstairs. It was a species unknown to us until then.

Lest I do Mrs. Colton an injustice, it should be said that our star classes were conducted outdoors—and at night—in her single concession to common sense. Mrs. Colton's inability to educate me, however, was unaffected by the setting. I never identified a star, either, and even constellations the size of the Big Dipper went unrecognized by me during the Colton years. Much later, when I was eighteen and my father and I were at a baseball game at Yankee Stadium, Mrs. Colton's name came up. "You poor son of a bitch," he commented. "She could have killed the love of nature in Audubon himself."

I had no way of knowing that these summers were being lived in a somewhat unusual atmosphere, although like any other boy my age, I was aware of certain yearnings not totally satisfied by my environment. One year, when I was eight or nine, I decided I wanted a lemonade stand. This entrepreneurial desire, filtering upwards, met with considerable enthusiasm, and Kiku was put in charge of the project.

Kiku was my grandparents' butler. He was the tallest Japanese I have ever known, standing well over six feet. Kiku's wardrobe—or the only part of it I ever saw—consisted of a severely tailored morning coat, starched white shirt, and black tie for informal daytime occasions; a dinner jacket for normal wear; and, if the assemblage exceeded six people, white tie and tails for evening. The only emotion I ever perceived in him was an abiding devotion to my grandfather, after whom he named his eldest son, Julius Rosenwald Yohamino. Upon my grandfather's death, Kiku returned to his homeland. During World War II it sometimes occurred to me that Julius Rosenwald Yohamino may well have had the oddest name in the entire Imperial Armed Forces of Japan.

In any case the date for the grand opening of the lemonade stand was set; I was to meet Kiku at ten A.M. at our family's entrance on Sheridan Road. Striding smartly up the gravel roadway, I arrived exactly on time for the commencement of my first job and found Kiku already on hand; we were, in fact, "open for business." Our stand consisted of a table covered by a beautiful damask cloth, a dozen large crystal glasses, two silver pitchers, pails of ice, and, to get to the heart of the matter, other pails filled to the brim with pure lemonade. The whole self-contained establishment, set up under a shade tree, was a testimonial to my grandfather's lifelong adage that to succeed you must give the customers something of true value. Kiku had wisely opted for his morning coat.

It was a hot, lazy Midwestern day, and although we had only the most discreet sign advertising our presence, the brisk traffic along Sheridan Road instantly noticed something special about our lemonade stand. We were a hit from the beginning, and we quickly established our business routine. When a customer stopped on our side of the road, Kiku filled a glass with ice and lemonade. I served it and collected the five cents. If the customer was going the other way, Kiku served it. That was because one of the hard and fast rules of the compound was that no one of my generation was allowed to cross Sheridan Road.

Like any other enterprise, this one had a few bugs to be ironed out. Several cars, for instance, departed with the crystal glasses, and we made a mental note to bring paper cups for those who were pressed for time—a custom not quite so prevalent then as now. Also, whenever we ran out of merchandise, Kiku had to make his way back to the Big House to refill the pails. Each of these trips meant that the stand was closed down for twenty to thirty minutes—quite a loss since Kiku could be spared only a few hours each day. I suggested that a third person bring on fresh lemonade pails at regular intervals, but three people for one lemonade stand was correctly judged to be a poor use of personnel. Oddly enough, it never occurred to a soul, including me, that it would have been sound business practice for me to gauge our lowering inventory and run and get the refills myself.

In spite of these minor problems, the enterprise was a bonanza. I kept all the nickels. Again, in retrospect, it seems too bad that I was never indoctrinated in the cost of doing business—i.e., Kiku's prorated salary, the price of the pure lemonade, and so on.

It was a joyous experience, but it was to be short-lived. A lady down the way on Sheridan Road had run a soft-drink stand for years. She was very nice; we all knew her. After one week she issued a plaintive plea that we were not only hurting her business but ruining it. If ever an antitrust action was justified it was hers. My grandfather instantly decided that the

Good Neighbor Policy should prevail, and we were ordered
to close down forthwith. My grandmother was delighted with
this turn of events since she had been far from pleased with
Kiku's long daily absences.

Looking back, I have only one great regret. It was hot work,
and during that week I drank enough lemonade to kill my taste
for the stuff to this day.

# ME

*and*

# THE CRIME
# OF THE CENTURY

MY MURDER WAS carefully planned by Nathan Leopold and Richard Loeb to take place in Chicago on May 21st, 1924. For some reason, this thought idly occurred to me some six decades later as I was dressing to attend a party marking my seventieth birthday. Or perhaps it was not really odd at all. That particular milestone is a natural time for reflection; to reach it, one has to be lucky enough to avoid the endless life-ending possibilities encountered steadily along the way. The fact that I lived to celebrate my seventieth birthday is proof, if proof is needed, that on this planet luck and timing are of vital importance. Indeed, I had arrived at the ripe old age of twelve only by the sheerest happenstance.

It was never a mystery to me why I was singled out as a prime prospect for this ghoulish crime. My grandfather, Julius Rosenwald, was for many decades the Chairman of Sears, Roebuck & Company. His great prominence made me an ideal choice for the Loeb-Leopold list of possible victims, especially since Richard Loeb's father was Sears's Senior Vice President. The two men lived one block apart and were driven to and from work together almost daily. Furthermore, Richard's younger brother and I were both students at the Harvard School for Boys, as was the tragically fated Bobby Franks. Because of all these circumstances, I knew Dickie Loeb casually even though he was nine years my senior.

My usual routine was to walk home from school. Had I followed it that day, I certainly would have hopped into the fateful Willys-Knight rented for the killing. This was even more likely because I was one of a group that took bird-watching instruction from Nathan Leopold on Jackson Park. As an ornithologist, he had impeccable credentials.

My seventieth-birthday party, given by two couples near and dear to my heart and attended by family members and warm friends, was an event that my wife and I will cherish forever. Yet the haunting thought that I might well have missed it by sixty years stayed with me the next morning and, in fact, increased in intensity. Although the celebration had taken place in New York City, I am a Southern California resident. I decided that, en route home, I would stop over in Chicago and look carefully at the area that marked my beginnings.

For an eleven-year-old boy, life seven decades ago in the Kenwood section of Chicago's South Side, our winter home, was quiet, even somewhat pastoral. Our infrequent sojourns downtown were limited to doctor appointments, great occasions worthy of a visit to the Chicago Theatre or a major restaurant, and State Street shopping expeditions. For the most part, however, our lives were lived in a pleasant small town surrounded by a vast, bustling city.

The northern outpost of my world was the apartment house at 45th Street and Woodlawn Avenue, where my brother and I lived with our parents. Walking one block west to Greenwood Avenue and heading south, one came to the Leopold home. Another block west was Ellis Avenue. Here, within a four-block area, were the Harvard School for Boys, my grandfather's mansion, and the lovely Loeb home, now destroyed but then almost directly across the street from the Franks' house.

Seeing the area again in the company of a lifelong friend, I was taken aback by its smallness. One can comfortably walk it in fifteen minutes. As I write this in the South of France and think of the earth as I have come to know it, it seems as if the world I knew as a child could be covered with a napkin. Loeb and Leopold committed not only a local crime but, more specifically, a neighborhood crime.

Occasionally, in the intervening years, I had returned to my grandfather's house, now long closed and untended. At one time it had served as headquarters for the now defunct Rosenwald Foundation. But because I had never before gone back with the inquiring eye that marked my latest visit, none of the things I now write about came to my mind. What a difference an inquiring eye makes as one goes through life, and how rarely most of us avail ourselves of it.

I was amazed at how wonderfully this portion of Kenwood had fared over the years. When I was a child it was lively; seventy years later the apartment houses and homes are still pleasant, with plentiful, well-tended garden space. All American cities are plagued by slums. This area, though quite a distance from the more fashionable North Side, seems a true oasis, a place environmentalists can savor.

The entire tour had a strong *déjà vu* motif, but pulling up to the entrance of the Harvard School for Boys made the years drop away. Although longtime memories can be treacherous, its red brick façade seemed identical to the one I had known, as did its compact, utilitarian interior. We had thought to steal an unnoticed glance and be on our way. However, classes were changing and, totally unprepared, we became the center of a small sea of interested, smiling faces. Now coeducational, integrated, and named the Harvard–St. George School, it seemed peopled with students dramatically different from those troublesome, apathetic sorts we read about and see on TV. A chorus of questions about the reason for our visit elicited the rather lame response from me that I went there long ago, the understatement of any season. As we left, I noticed the administrative office. There, probably in some archive, lay the records of the school's two most famous pupils: Nathan Leopold and Robert Franks.

Driving south, one comes quickly to Jackson Park, beautiful and verdant then and now, and the scene of many of Nathan Leopold's bird classes. Looking benignly down on its quiet beauty for the past fifty-plus years has been the Museum of Science and Industry, my grandfather's gift to the city he loved and, I am told, the most widely attended museum on earth. It is beyond comprehension that the two young men who burst upon the world scene to achieve such infamous immortality were spawned in this peaceful, prospering Kenwood enclave.

They were distinguished from their neighbors' children principally by their brilliance. Dickie Loeb attended U-High; Babe Leopold went to Harvard School. Both skipped grades seemingly at random, graduating from high school at fifteen. Both enrolled at the University of Chicago but transferred to the University of Michigan. There they roomed together briefly and, although they had known each other for years, it was at this point that their friendship took root and they grew to recognize traits in one another that were to bind them together, even after Leopold returned to the U. of C. Graduating Phi Beta Kappa at an age when other boys were getting high-school diplomas, they were clearly marked for distinguished futures.

Leopold possessed the far greater intellectual capacity. In addition to being an ornithologist, he was multilingual, having studied fifteen languages and mastered five. He read widely and became a disciple of the Nietzschean superman theory. His curious, searching mind was always discovering new spheres of interest.

Loeb's mind was bright, quick, and superficial; it certainly was more than sufficient to keep him at the top in scholastic attainment. Handsome and attractive, he was a facile conversationalist to whom lying came as naturally as telling the truth. Fully aware of these characteristics, he used them constantly and skillfully to create a persona that made his participation in the Franks murder as incomprehensible as that of Leopold.

The widely supported theory that Loeb craved a slave figure and Leopold a master helps explain their special relationship, as does their sexuality, in those days a shocking piece of the total fabric of the crime. Homosexuality was neither accepted nor discussed seventy years ago, and the fact that these two well-born boys practiced it, with others and between themselves, was, in and of itself, mind-boggling.

It was inevitable that this macabre murder, its detection, and the trial would create a media extravaganza that spread beyond the United States. Sensational press coverage drew throngs to the courthouse, where, in turn, newspaper cameras photographed mounted police holding back the crowds. Emotions were inflamed, and the demand for hanging was overwhelming. The killers, both Jewish, had chosen a Jewish victim—otherwise, righteous public indignation, combined with Ku Klux Klan leaderhip, might well have resulted in race riots. The anti-Semitic Klan, then active in the Midwest, would have gravitated naturally to this made-to-order cause. But the fact that the crime was motiveless made it unique, and that's why it fascinates people to this day. For the facts surrounding the case, I have drawn primarily on newspaper articles of the time and on two books: Hal Higdon's *The Crime of the Century: The Leopold and Loeb Case* and Irving Stone's *Darrow for the Defense*.

Perhaps nothing in this quintessential horror story is more bloodcurdling than that these two pampered young adults conceived and, over a six-month period, carefully plotted to murder a fellow human being without once experiencing doubt, pity, or remorse. No testimony or interviews indicate that these feelings ever marred their early skull sessions, where potential victims, including me, were evaluated, murder techniques and body disposal minutely discussed, and follow-up tactics carefully planned.

The cruelty of cutting short a life, and the tragic effect on the victim's family, did not occur to them. Since the murder was intended to remain forever unsolved, they naturally gave no thought to the suffering of their own families. The act would simply be the ultimate tribute to their brilliance, a statement that, as superior beings, they were not bound by the conventions that regulated the behavior of other mortals.

Less than a year later, when Loeb and Leopold were standing trial for this "perfect" crime, spectators, press, and attorneys alike were aghast at the number of times they snickered, giggled, and exchanged knowing glances. They seemed genuinely surprised, even contemptuous, over the waves of revulsion that regularly swept the courtroom. That kind of understanding was, from birth to death, denied them, and this was the basic difference between them and others.

The distinguished actor-photographer Roddy McDowall, a veteran of hundreds of roles, played Richard Loeb in the 1957 Broadway production of *Compulsion*. Never, he told me, had he found it more difficult to get a handle on a part. He had researched his subject carefully but was well into rehearsals before he realized what the key was: Horror, revulsion, and remorse were never a part of Dickie's thinking. Once McDowall knew that he must play the part as a lark, his troubles were over—except that he was depressed at every performance, playing with the actors who portrayed family members.

These two bad seeds hardly arrived at the perfect-murder concept as newcomers to crime. Far from it. Behind them stretched a series of unlawful acts so long and varied that there was some justification in their unswerving belief that getting caught was the private preserve of fools. Some of these crimes were confessed during the trial. In other instances, clues were unwittingly revealed that put the finishing touches on other unsolved cases. Since they were never prosecuted for these crimes, the evidence against them in every instance is technically circumstantial but, in many cases, compelling beyond doubt.

Their brilliance, wealth, and social status served as a shield of unbelievable effectiveness. Today that would be impossible; the authorities are too crime-wise and cynical. Seventy years ago, however, whenever a clue pointed in their direction it was immediately dropped, on the grounds that it was unthinkable and therefore obviously the result of faulty deduction. Even the interrogation in the Franks case was briefly hampered by obsequious, apologetic questioning. If it had not been for the existence of totally damning and conclusive evidence, it is conceivable that they might have slipped through the net.

Their earliest criminality, which in some instances did not involve both of them, ran the gamut, beginning with almost prankish minor thefts. A series of burglaries of college fraternity houses followed, and then several cases of arson. Finally, in the web of mystery that will forever surround Loeb and Leopold, there were almost certainly several other murders. The solution to one crime in particular, involving castration, was there for the taking. In that case, a suit brought against them after two years of imprisonment was settled out of court by their families.

The Franks murder was conceived and executed out of frustration. None of their crimes up to that time had brought Loeb and Leopold either the thrill or the attention they longed for. This act, performed within the confines of their home base upon a member of their affluent neighborhood clan, would provide both sexual fulfillment and media coverage. A ransom demand for $10,000 would be integral, serving as a paper trail leading away from them. After all, they were known among their peers as having the largest allowances and the most lenient fathers, who gave them money without question, enabling them to gamble for high stakes, plan trips to Europe, and do whatever else they wished. At one point, as things began to close in on them, my grandfather, upset at Mr. Loeb's anguish, went to the courthouse and told the authorities that it was probably foolish to ascribe this dreadful crime, obviously committed for ransom, to two boys who had everything.

It was widely rumored that Dickie Loeb had shown his hand early in life. His family had a palatial summer home in Charlevoix, Michigan, where each year a tutor was engaged for him. One summer his tutor hesitantly reported to Richard's father that the boy tortured and killed birds and small animals. Dickie, handsome and bright, was the apple of his father's eye, and it was instantly clear to Mr. Loeb that he had been guilty of engaging a mentor who was a liar, and perhaps even crazy. The tutor was immediately discharged.

Inevitably, the weeks and months of careful planning were concluded. All was in order, every exigency covered. The day of execution inexorably arrived. On May 21st, 1924, Babe and Dickie, in their rented Willys-Knight, cruised around the Harvard School for Boys looking for the one element needed to complete their plan—a victim. By that time, the decision had been made to broaden the list of acceptable candidates, and the name of fourteen-year-old Robert Franks was among them.

These two older boys, whom he knew and trusted, picked him up a little more than halfway home on his three-block walk from school, between 49th and 50th streets on Ellis Avenue. He rode in the front seat. Who drove and who sat in the back remains one of the many mysteries of the case. Both steadfastly claimed to be the driver.

The car turned east at the next corner, and, probably less than a block from his home, Bobby was hit over the head from the rear seat with a heavy chisel. After additional blows, his body was pushed and tugged to the backseat, where still more blows almost certainly ended his life then and there.

Shoving him onto the floor and covering his body with a rug, Leopold and Loeb turned south and drove into Indiana. Following their plan, they cruised the streets near Hammond for some hours with the body on the floor, waiting for night to fall. If ever there was a time when revulsion might have assailed them, this should have been it. The record fails to show it. It does show, however, that they got hungry and bought sandwiches, which they ate in the car, and that they used some of this time to partially disrobe the corpse.

When darkness came, they stopped in a marshy area close to Wolf Lake. Completing the disrobing, they dragged their victim to a nearby culvert and, covering his body with hydrochloric acid to make identification more difficult, shoved him in headfirst. The state's attorney later claimed sexual molestation, but it was never proved. At the culvert a pair of glasses fell out of Leopold's pocket, sealing the murderers' fate as certainly as they had sealed the doom of the boy. Furthermore, they left Franks' feet protruding from the culvert, leading to the discovery of the body and the glasses within twenty-four hours.

During that period Babe and Dickie followed their game plan, which included the clumsy, amateurish series of ransom notes and phone calls that added to the agony of the parents. The notes were eventually traced to a stolen typewriter in Nathan's room, but by that time no further proof was needed.

On May 29th, eight days after the crime, the glasses were traced to Nathan Leopold. The fashionable optician Almer Coe & Company always placed an identifying mark on its glasses. This pair bore that mark. Only three people had this precise frame. The other two had airtight alibis. Even under these damning circumstances, Leopold still wriggled glibly and persuasively, explaining that he must have dropped the glasses on a bird-watching expedition.

The trap was closed, however, and on May 31st, State's Attorney Robert E. Crowe took separate confessions from both. Each claimed that the other had conceived the idea and committed the actual murder.

Clarence Darrow, Chicago's great defense lawyer, was awakened after midnight on June 2nd by the incessant ringing of his doorbell. His four unwelcome, extremely agitated visitors, led by Dickie's uncle, a friend of the Darrow family, pleaded with him to save the lives of the two boys. Money, they said, was no object.

Darrow's deep, abiding conviction that the death penalty in and of itself constituted murder by the state was the cornerstone of his life. He had grown older than his sixty-seven years defending and saving the lives of more than one hundred convicted murderers. Almost invariably the crowd and the press had stood against him. Defending this vile murder, he knew, would heap upon him abuse beyond anything he had ever known. He pointed out that the Bachrach brothers, excellent attorneys related to the Loebs, had already been retained for the defense.

But finally the hope that saving Nathan and Richard from the gallows would strike a blow against capital punishment proved irresistible to him. He accepted the case and received a $10,000 retainer. His fee was not discussed.

He had underestimated the outcry, led by the press, that was raised against him. The poor and defenseless, to whom he had devoted a lifetime, accused him of selling out. Other attorneys reviled him, saying that he had set back the practice of criminal law by decades. But, having made his decision, he pressed on with the preparation of his case. Perhaps his most difficult accomplishment was the reuniting of his two clients. Because of the acrimony between them, brought on by the contempt each felt for the other's statements, denials, and accusations, they seemed irreconcilable. Darrow was probably the only person capable of convincing them that if they did not hang together they would surely hang separately.

Prosecutor Crowe, no doubt feeling like the proverbial cat that had swallowed the canary, also prepared. Not even the prospect of facing the mighty Darrow seemed to faze him. After all, Loeb and Leopold had confessed to the crime in the greatest detail. The sentencing was all that remained, and one had only to talk to people and read the papers to be aware of the emotions that gripped Chicago. It would be impossible to find twelve good men and true who would not want execution. Certain promotion, and perhaps high state office, beckoned the man into whose lap this plum had dropped.

On May 31st, State's Attorney Crowe told the press that Loeb and Leopold had revealed my selection as the primary victim. This revelation was highlighted in the June 1st newspapers. The *Daily News* ran a front-page picture of my grandfather, grandmother, and mother with the bold caption "Her Son Escaped."

How had I escaped? Instead of walking home as usual, I was picked up at school by the family chauffeur because I had a dental appointment. When one measures the number of my dental appointments against the number of days in the school year, the odds against me were so formidable that no self-respecting Las Vegas gambler would have made book on it. While not partial to dentists, since then I have always viewed the breed with an understandable tolerance.

My parents reacted swiftly to the news of my involvement. My copy of the daily papers was stripped down, reduced to the sports section. This ploy went unnoticed by me, since that was the only section I ever read. I was, and have remained all my life, a rabid baseball fan and could not then imagine another reason for publishing a newspaper. Rereading the papers of the period, I noted that on the 20th of May, the day before the killing and the last normal day Chicago was to experience for a long time, the White Sox beat the Boston Red Sox, 2–1, behind the stellar pitching of Hollis Thurston and with the help of two hits from the bat of Harry Hooper. Those names, along with such stars as Collins and Schalk, are all clear and verdant to me to this day. The paper, it might be worth noting, cost two cents.

I was immediately taken out of school, and our family moved several weeks ahead of schedule to our summer home in the Ravinia section of Highland Park. Then the possessor of a totally uninquiring nature, I never questioned this action. After all, who in his right mind would object to leaving school a few weeks early?

In Ravinia I was never alone, but this was accomplished in so casual a fashion that the word "bodyguard" did not enter my vocabulary. During the course of the summer, I was told about the murder in such vague and general terms that I probably knew less of the horror and the trial than anyone else. My rather secluded summer lifestyle contributed greatly to the success of all this careful orchestration.

In the fall I was switched from the Harvard School to the University of Chicago Laboratory School, probably in an attempt at anonymity. Ironically, it was a change from Leopold's alma mater to Loeb's. On my first day, a new classmate asked for and received my autograph. I suppose this seemed odd to me, but, preoccupied with the new school, I did not dwell on it. It was, however, a first, for this heinous crime and my association with it were to remain forever a part of my life. Not, of course, autographs, and not constantly, but never too far below the surface. To this day, people occasionally ask me if it was true, usually saying they had heard it and could not believe it.

At times, as with the 1956 publication of Meyer Levin's book *Compulsion,* it naturally flared up. I remember playing golf with Jack Benny about that time. Afterward, over a drink, he said very seriously, "I just can't believe you were the one they planned to kill." An avid but mediocre golfer, I replied, "The way I putted today, I wish they'd gotten me." He roared, and for some years quoted me so regularly that I was sometimes asked if I had said it.

Another time, over a casual disagreement during dinner, the witty and urbane publisher Bennett Cerf commented earnestly, "Loeb and Leopold certainly got the wrong guy!"

For the most part, the inquiries about my connection with the crime stem from idle curiosity, and they prove only that after all these years, despite the fact that murder is today regrettably more commonplace, this particular subhuman act has not been forgotten.

On June 6th, sixteen days after the crime, a murder indictment was handed down. The trial began before Judge John B. Caverly on July 21st.

From start to finish, State's Attorney Crowe was in the position of a good club fighter up against Joe Louis. Darrow's initial blow was a stunning one from which his opponent never really recovered. He agreed completely with Crowe that it would be impossible to find a jury that would not vote for hanging, and he knew that Crowe's entire battle plan was based on a jury trial. The moment the trial started, he changed the arraignment plea from "not guilty by reason of insanity" to "guilty." This legal maneuver entitled him to waive a trial by jury. Now the decision would be entirely in the hands of the court.

But Darrow had grave doubts. Judge Caverly, known as a

competent but undistinguished jurist, was certainly not on record as opposing the death penalty. Caught, however, between a slim chance and no chance, Darrow never hesitated. As witness followed witness, he kept picking up points against the people's lawyer. Eminent psychiatrists appeared for both sides. Psychiatry was relatively new, and this was perhaps the first famous testing ground for the still-raging controversy as to the value of such testimony. Darrow insisted that these experts canceled one another out. He constantly stressed the youth of his clients and his belief that killing by the state was murder.

He was brilliant, but he had considerable help from his opponent. Crowe kept insisting that Franks had been murdered for ransom by two high-stakes gamblers deep in debt and afraid to admit it to their parents. That argument did not wash, even with the vast majority who favored the death penalty. And then, to cap the climax, as the trial reached its dénouement Crowe inadvertently made a derogatory statement about the court that so angered Judge Caverly that he rebuked him from the bench.

The difference between these two attorneys reminds me of something my grandfather said when asked privately why Sears enjoyed far greater success than its archrival, Montgomery Ward. "Hard work," he answered, "and Sewell Avery," an expression of his lack of respect for Ward's chairman.

In concluding, Darrow stated firmly that he and the two families agreed that his clients should be completely separated from society, without appeal, for the rest of their lives. The thirty-two-day trial ended August 28th, and on September 10th the court ruled in favor of Darrow and life sentences. One day later Loeb and Leopold rode together to prison in Joliet.

For seven months, Darrow, exhausted by the trial, heard nothing from either family. All attempts to communicate with them concerning his fee were unavailing. The bar assocation asked Darrow to permit it to name the amount of the fee and collect it. Darrow refused. Finally, Richard Loeb's uncle, the same man who had said, "Money is no object," appeared at Darrow's office. He announced that he was prepared to pay $100,000, less the $10,000 retainer already spent in the preparation of the case, to be divided among Darrow and the two

Bachrach brothers. And so it was that the man who was rumored in the press to be getting a million-dollar fee actually
received, and signed a release for, $30,000.

Loeb's life sentence was terminated after twelve years of
imprisonment. He was stabbed to death in the shower by James
Day, a life prisoner resisting Dickie's homosexual advances.
The nature and frequency of these attacks resulted in a county
jury's finding Day not guilty. It was a fitting end for Dickie,
whose thirty-one-year life span was a constant, tragic rejection
of the advantages handed him at birth. The prison cell that
served as his home when he died was smaller than a linen closet
in the house where he had lived out his nineteen years of
freedom. His legacy was murder and many irreparably broken
lives. The legendary reporter Edwin A. Lahey wrote of his
demise, "Richard Loeb, who was a master of the English language, today ended a sentence with a proposition."

"Nathan Leopold will break after five years in prison." So
pronounced an eminent psychiatrist in a featured newspaper
story, as the sentence of life plus ninety-nine years started.
Wrong by 180 degrees. Babe's adaptation to prison life began
at the beginning and never wavered. Confinement, transfers
to different prisons, and the wear and tear of life behind bars
all failed to undermine his adjustment. No negative reports
marred his record. He upgraded prison libraries and, in 1945,
participated in malaria experiments. As in a motion picture
montage, the days turned into weeks, months, years, and decades. The phrase "model prisoner" began to filter outside the
walls. Spread by activist groups opposed to severe sentencing
and, no doubt, by skillful family-inspired propaganda, this
description, based on the truth, gained momentum.

In 1949 the parole board reduced Leopold's sentence to life
plus eighty-five years, making him eligible for parole in 1953.
It was a definite light at the end of the tunnel. But his parole
requests were denied in 1953, 1955, and 1956, the year Meyer
Levin's novel was published. It sold 130,000 hardcover copies.
Most readers were appalled by the book. Inexplicably, however, it increased the drumbeat for clemency. The following
year the smell of parole was in the air. The family knew it,
and before the Broadway production of *Compulsion* opened

they arranged for their lawyers to preview the play. McDowall vividly recalls the "eerie performance at the Erlanger Theatre, empty except for three attorneys." They demanded and got several script changes.

On March 13th, 1958, Nathan Leopold finally was paroled. He left for Puerto Rico the next day, to become an X-ray technician. Thirty-four years had passed since the murder of Robert Franks. Darrow's eloquent statement that his clients should never rejoin society, a major factor in beating the death sentence, had long been forgotten.

I was asked quite often how I felt about this turn of events. Since I mistakenly pictured Leopold as performing worthwhile work strictly in Puerto Rico, it did not disturb me. Years later, by the merest chance, I learned that his movements were far from restricted. He was permitted to travel and came frequently to Chicago to visit relatives and friends. Obviously these trips gave him pleasure, an emotion largely denied Robert Franks' parents from the day of their son's death.

The realization that a sentence of life plus ninety-nine years provided no insurance against ultimate release affected me profoundly. It was, after all, Leopold who had said in a newspaper interview prior to his trial, "A thirst for knowledge justifies any cruelty; a six-year-old boy is justified in pulling the wings from a fly if by doing so he learns the fly is helpless." He lived free for thirteen years that were highlighted by a marriage and a lawsuit against the author of *Compulsion,* and died of natural causes in 1971. I changed from an individual basically indifferent to the continuing capital-punishment debate to a strong proponent. The intervening years have only strengthened this view.

After the sentencing, there were many editorials stating that the only way to alleviate crime was to get at the root causes. Seventy years later, the same thing is being said. It would seem that the more things change, the more they remain depressingly the same. In some areas there has actually been retrogression. Following their confession, Loeb and Leopold were tried and sentenced with what must be regarded as remarkable speed compared with the snail-like trial system that prevails today. John Hinckley, Jr., who attempted to assassinate the President of the United States on television, was able to avoid trial long enough to provide a strange twist to Justice Oliver Wendell Holmes's view that justice delayed is justice denied.

Both Nathan and Richard were classic examples of the moral expressed in Paul Bourget's famous novel *The Disciple,* in which he speaks of "young men who sneer at distinction between good and evil and indulge all their whims and caprices and with Nietzsche talk of living dangerously and seeking risk and adventure at any cost." That, in a nutshell, was their credo. It is a tragedy that they did not live their lives instead by the old proverb "Be very careful what you set your heart upon. You are almost sure to get it."

# ME

*and*

# MY TRUE LOVE OF THE GREAT AMERICAN PASTIME

Burt Lancaster, playing old Doc in the dream-fable baseball film *A Field of Dreams,* is interviewed by Ray, played by Kevin Costner. The script reads:

RAY

When you got to the Majors you played only one inning of one game. What happened in that inning?

DOC

It was the last day of the season, bottom of the 8th. John McGraw points a bony finger at me and says, "Right field." Well, sir, I jumped up like I was sitting on a spring and ran out onto the field.

RAY

Did you get to make a play?

DOC

Nope. They never hit the ball out of the infield. The game ended and the season was over. I knew they were going to send me back down so I hung 'em up.

RAY

And what was it like?

DOC

It was like coming this close to your dreams and then watching them brush past you like a stranger in a crowd.

Very few American boys ever get as far as Doc. Millions, however, dream of just once coming to bat in a packed Major League stadium, getting some wood on the ball, and running out a hit to the cheers of the crowd. The dream may fade with time, but it rarely dies. Baseball is too integral a part of our American dream and heritage.

The late Commissioner of Baseball, A. Bartlett Giamatti, who was also the President of Yale University, said, "Baseball is one of the free-standing institutions that has survived without radical changes since before the Civil War. It's one of the things that keeps the country together." I agree with the Commissioner, the greatest friend the game ever had. I am a minuscule part of the base that permits baseball to survive. I am a fan; in fact, a third-generation box-seat fan and proof positive that in the Grand Old Game only the players grow old.

My grandfather used his season box frequently until the World Series of 1919. That was the year gamblers bribed eight members of the brilliant, shamefully underpaid Chicago White Sox to throw the World Series to Cincinnati. That these particular idols had feet of clay was almost too much to bear, particularly in Chicago. A front page *Chicago Tribune* cartoon depicted a ragged urchin watching the brilliant, illiterate young "Black Sox" outfielder, Shoeless Joe Jackson, walking up the courthouse steps. The caption read, "Say it ain't so, Joe," a phrase that has remained in our language. My grandfather never entered a baseball stadium again. Several years later his chauffeur saw a famous "Black Sox" pitcher in the street, got out of his car, and spat in his face.

The eight wrongdoers were banished for life. The gamblers who welched on their deal with the players emerged unscathed. The penurious owner, Charles Comiskey, who made the players ripe picking for bribes, owned the team until his death.

My father took me to my first baseball game at Comiskey Park in 1921. I did not know that the national pastime was still in a state of trauma, but I knew instantly that I loved the game, and Comiskey Park as well. It was, after all, less than ten years old and properly hailed as a baseball palace. It remained the home of the White Sox until the end of the 1990 season when, old and much the worse for wear, it kept a rendezvous with the wrecking ball.

The Chicago press and the fans dredged up every good memory that the teams and the Park had contributed to the glory of the game. This took a bit of doing since the franchise's highwater marks were few and far between. I am happy that I have outlasted the stadium, but sad that through its life its name remained unchanged. Furthermore, the spanking new edifice that opens next season will be known as the new Comiskey Park. He deserved no such tribute. It was Comiskey and a handful of men like him who ignited the mutual distrust between owners and players that is a root cause of the strikes that come up every four or five years.

A few members of the 1919 team played their hearts out and were never implicated. I saw them play often over the next few years. When I left Chicago at age thirteen for New York via Paris my love affair with the game was firmly in place. Qualifications for membership are many. True fans do not wait to become involved until World Series time. The ebb and flow of so-called "routine" games is meat and drink. The successes and failures over the long season mirror our own. The off-season hiatus is an annual period of discontent. My friend Billy Wilder, the famous film director, thinks this time presents an ideal oppotunity to become involved in cryonics, leaving careful instructions to be unfrozen when the teams arrive at spring training. My own way of coping is less risky: I simply talk a great deal about baseball. My every word sparkles with authority. I know that much of it is inaccurate but it sustains me.

I have initially disliked every change that has been made in the game. When night baseball started I felt that the end had come. Now I love it and cannot conceive of the game without it. I regarded AstroTurf as an abomination, and still dislike it. Domed stadiums are an intrusion on baseball's natural habitat, but I have developed a lofty tolerance for them since they permit baseball to be played in cities with inclement weather. I railed against the growing power of TV and baseball having to "knuckle under" on the starting times of World Series games. To continue to rail at this fact of life is the height of futility and, in addition, I have found more advantages than disadvantages from it. The medium will be relieved to know that I am not fighting it. My resentment and anger remain high about the designated pinch hitter, an American League abomination which truly tampers with the purity of the game.

No love affair is a totally smooth ride. The owners and the players should long ago have worked out a less acrimonious method to handle the issues that divide them, since this bitterness represents a very real threat to the game. At the time of the 1985 strike I wrote a letter to the sports editor of the *Los Angeles Times,* pompously stating that "the fans have the ultimate right to strike" and that I would never use my seats again. I was thrilled when the strike ended, and used my tickets regularly. I felt even angrier at the conclusion of the 1990 strike, but I was wise enough by then to know that I would never give up my tickets. The sight of the grass and the diamond, the special taste of the hot dogs, the grace, flow, and drama of the plays, make such a drastic action impossible. In addition, there is the unadulterated pleasure of harmless hero-worship. It is only normal to put on a pedestal a player who hits a key home run or pitches a no-hit game. Even if they had a Center to Break the Baseball Habit I would not enroll. It makes me too happy. I have read a great deal about efforts to shorten the game, usually by sportswriters who want to get their work done. I have never heard such heresy from a fan.

During the decades I lived in New York the city was a movable baseball feast and I participated joyously. The imperial Yankees marched from pennant to pennant. Babe Ruth, Lou Gehrig, and Joe DiMaggio became legends before they were halfway through their playing careers. The Giants of the Polo Grounds above Coogan's Bluff had some superb players and were a mecca for older fans loyal to the memory of John McGraw. Finally, there were the Brooklyn Dodgers of Ebbets Field, evolving from clowns to greatness under Branch Rickey and later Walter O'Malley, who was to become my close friend.

My father knew Babe Ruth, and I, hopelessly overawed, met him two or three times. "Hello, kid," he would say, which is how he greeted everyone, including most of his teammates. Only a handful of people were known to him by name.

Today, suspension of athletes for drug abuse, unknown in that more innocent era, fills the sports pages. The only unfavorable publicity that the Babe received was because of his voracious appetite. He regularly ate two or three hot dogs out of public view during a game. Once he enjoyed fifteen and had to have his stomach pumped. He was briefly suspended and that was trumpeted in the press. His womanizing and lack of training were hushed up, although his road roommate said that he roomed with an empty suitcase. The press, however, felt no obligation to publicize the flaws of these sometimes less-than-perfect heroes.

These three teams were so different that for a long time I played no favorites, although rooting for a specific team is one of the hallmarks of a true fan. I was, however, deeply involved in the great hot-stove league topic of the day entitled, "Who is the best center fielder in New York?" I rated them:

1. Mays—Giants
2. Mantle—Yankees
3. Snider—Dodgers

This often acrimonious debate was a very close second to team partisanship. I finally got back on track by opting for the colorful Brooklyn Dodgers, mainly because of Leo Durocher, their exciting, controversial manager. He had been for many years a feisty, good fielding shortstop. I got to know him around the night life of the city and we became friends.

Competitive almost to a fault, stretching to win was an integral part of his character. In a golf game involving a two-dollar wager he would cough or yell "Watchit" during his opponent's backswing. In Ping-Pong he would serve too quickly and would loudly announce incorrect scores in his favor. Yet he was fun, vital, exciting, and a repository of baseball lore.

On the field his opponents were his mortal enemies. He loudly questioned their talent, character, and ancestry. He gloated when an umpire was hit by a pitched ball. "Does it hurt?" he would yell happily.

He stretched his baseball talents almost to the breaking point with his indomitable spirit. A friend said of him, "No light hitting shortstop ever went further." Durocher-managed teams scored stunning, memorable World Series victories. The phrase he coined about a rival manager, "Nice guys finish last," furnishes a key to his character.

I often had the use of Leo's Ebbets Field box. The park was

so small that it was simple to talk to him from these seats in a conversational tone. One day I said as he passed by, "Leo, you kept that pitcher in too long." Eyes blazing, he approached his box and responded, "Shut up, goddamn it. You watch the game and let me manage the team."

Many of his friends sat in his box, including the film star George Raft. Raft not only played gangster roles but associated with dubious characters. Leo's flamboyance made him a target. Eventually the Commissioner, a mediocre choice, barred Durocher from baseball for a year for consorting with these people. It was, in my opinion, a classic example of guilt by association, a seat-of-the-pants judgment that discredited baseball. No effort was made to determine whether the usage of these seats by these people was in any way harmful. If inside tips or betting were involved, Durocher should have been barred for life. If not, he should at the very worst been asked for the sake of appearances to use better judgment in disposing of his box.

The Office of the Commissioner has traveled light-years since then, as witness the thorough, dispassionate methods used in separating Pete Rose, a player, and George Steinbrenner, an owner, from the game.

Durocher survived this low blow and returned to new triumphs. However, it made me realize that my friend could be susceptible to events that might harm his career. Babe Ruth is alleged to have said when Leo broke in as a Yankee rookie that "this kid leads the League in stolen sweaters."

The highlight of Durocher's managing career was having Willie Mays play for him. The presence of a superstar of that magnitude on the roster is something most managers only dream about. Durocher had enough sense to leave him alone; there is no point in tinkering with a natural. He made one exception, however, which further glorified the circus catches that dotted Mays' career. The manager kept drilling it into him: "Willie, when you get the ball, throw it back into the infield. It's not helping anyone out there." Mays, who idolized Durocher, quickly added this weapon to his arsenal, to the discomfort of opposing base runners.

Eventually Leo failed to arrive at a contract with Walter

O'Malley and migrated like a homing pigeon to Hollywood. He became the friend of film stars who earned in a month what he earned in a year. He accepted a Hollywood agent's advice to never manage again unless he owned a part of the team. It was an impossible demand. No offers came his way. These events did him irretrievable, self-inflicted damage, but he was pleased that his exploits were amusing to his new fair-weather friends.

He was once held up at gunpoint in his Beverly Hills garage. He told his young assailants that they were crazy to take the few hundred dollars he had in his pocket and suggested they come in, where he would give them money from his safe. Once in his house he sat and talked with them about baseball and the folly of their ways. They left with an autograph, two tickets to a game, and no money. Perhaps he reformed them.

Leo, who had long since withdrawn his exorbitant demands, began to complain that he was the victim of blacklisting. Walter O'Malley finally got him back into baseball as the Dodgers' third-base coach with the proviso that he never second-guess Walter Alston, the manager. He broke that covenant almost immediately, but Alston was secure enough to be tolerant of him. He went on to manage the Houston Astros but it was never quite the same. It was an exciting career, but Leo and baseball should have been kinder to each other.

In 1946 I moved to Los Angeles, temporarily I believed, to take a job in the motion picture business. I was certain that I would miss Big League Baseball and the Dodgers abysmally. I was right. There was no television, and I remember driving to the top of a mountain one afternoon to faintly hear on my car radio the live play-by-play broadcast of a crucial Dodger game played in St. Louis.

I never dreamed that a decade later the team would follow me to California. Everything prior to that point had been Minor League training to prepare me to become a devout Los Angeles Dodger fan.

Dodger owner Walter O'Malley, sole architect of baseball's migration to the West Coast, was a colorful Irishman and proud of it. On the golf course he would blithely kick the ball from under a tree out onto the fairway with the remark, "Any Irishman worth his salt knows that his best club is his foot." He loved winning. The Dodgers' consistent winning record and high attendance were proof positive of his skills. Rich owners who regarded their team as a hobby found it difficult to compete with him.

Walter was at his desk by nine A.M. and stayed through the night home games. Very little went on that he didn't know about. Eyes twinkling, cigar ever present, he loved to ruminate. He once told Roger Kahn, the great baseball chronicler, that the key to the Dodgers' drawing power was that the restrooms were clean. It was a typical O'Malley oversimplification, but it cut to the heart of his philosophy. He insisted that Dodger Stadium be a sparklingly clean family place with ticket prices as low as possible. He trained his son Peter in that tradition.

If he was a despot, as sometimes charged, he was a benevolent one who consistently ran the finest sports franchise in the country. Baseball players have regarded their years in Dodger Blue as a career highlight. An astute picker of people, the team has had only two field managers in thirty years. The turbulent Steinbrenner Yankees had that many every year. The comparative results speak for themselves. The Dodgers look after their own. From the moment the Hall of Fame catcher Roy Campanella was found under a car, hopelessly crippled, the Dodgers have stood behind him quietly, generously and unfailingly supportive. That is only the most highly visible example of their policy.

Only a man of Walter's ability and wily persistence could have withstood the roadblocks that some members of the Los Angeles City Council tried to put in his way to scuttle his planned move west. This has always amazed me. When Walter first took me on a tour of Chavez Ravine there were goats running around this unused land where Dodger Stadium, a bonanza to the city of Los Angeles, now stands surrounded by verdant planting. City government is indeed, as the King of Siam would have said, "a puzzlement."

It must have required every bit of his blarney to persuade the late Horace Stoneham, owner of the New York Giants, to move into the San Francisco wind tunnel known as Candlestick Park. Without a second team on the West Coast, O'Malley's dream would not have been feasible.

Brooklyn citizenry has not forgiven the man who took their beloved "bums" away. However, at the other end of America he found a populace starving to become a Major League city. Perhaps the Los Angeles water disagreed with the highly touted Dodgers of 1958. They had a dreadful year. The following season they won the World Series and the heart of the city. They have never lost it.

The most valuable part of the Dodger franchise that came west with Walter was not the famous players that were transplanted, although they brought glitz to the mix. That honor belongs to the Dodger Hall of Fame broadcaster, Vince Scully. Walter was well aware of it from the beginning. "These fans," he told me early on, "are eager to learn some of the fine points of big-league baseball. Vinny is the perfect teacher." I agreed completely, but assumed that he was not including me, a seasoned, knowledgeable fan. How wrong I was! Although Scully is naturally a rabid Dodger fan, he keeps it secret. He feels his job is to describe the game rather than to be a partisan rooter. No fan wants a sports telecast or broadcast to be a schoolroom. Scully's success is that game after game is described in an entertaining way, with nuggets of baseball knowledge and lore inserted in a way that adds enjoyment while producing knowledgeable fans. Recently Jim Murray, the Pulitzer Prize–winning Los Angeles Times sports columnist, wrote, "Once an umpire named Beans Riorden barked to an impatient manager, 'It ain't nothin' 'til I say what it is.'" Thirty-five years of Dodger fans can say, "It ain't nothin' 'til Scully tells us what it is." I have never brought a desire for true scholarship to my status as a fan, but I have absorbed by osmosis enough of what Scully has offered me to add to my enjoyment of the game. Fandom's desire to become scholars of the sport is amazingly emphasized by George Wills' landmark book, Men at Work, which topped the New York Times nonfiction Best Seller List for many weeks. I submit that a book even of this superior quality on any other sport could not come close to the popularity of Men at Work.

Shortly after the Dodgers' arrival, a close friend challenged my claim to being a true fan. "No one," he claimed, "qualifies who has never sat in the bleachers." I argued that it is a myth that bleacherites are the best fans. Shortly afterward we gave it a try. I was amazed at how much I enjoyed it, and have always sat in the bleachers several times each season. I quickly came to the conclusion that bleacherites are better fans. From the bleachers one sees the ball park from the opposite perspective, but it is just as beautiful. Bleacherites may not be too knowledgeable about catchers, but they certainly have deep, vociferous feelings about outfielders. There is no stronger love affair in the game than that between an outstanding home-team outfielder and his bleacherites. They are more closely bonded than we are in the plush Stadium Club level. They are more cohesive and have a purer love of the game.

I do not pretend, however, that I have any complaints. I selected my box under Walter's watchful eye months before the stadium opened. Until Jack Benny's death, we shared the box. He was one of my closest friends and a sheer joy. Jack loved baseball. While he was still perfectly well, he said to me at a game, "I'd hate to die because then we couldn't go to any more games together." I said, "Jack, if you die I don't want to go to any more games with you because I don't want to join you." He was the only comedian I ever knew who genuinely loved the humor of other people, and his uproarious laugh was typical of him. He was a diabetic and at almost every game he would say to me, "I'm gonna get some ice cream, but please don't tell Mary." I assured him that I wouldn't tell her, but always asked if his doctors wouldn't catch on to it at his weekly examination. "I'm not afraid of the doctors," he said. "I'm just afraid of Mary."

Autograph seekers were ever present and he was always obliging. It was a distraction, and one day I complained about it mildly. "Listen," he said, "if these people didn't ask me for my autograph I couldn't afford these seats." He told me that years ago he was in Miami for a vacation. His total lack of privacy forced him to fly to a small Caribbean island where no one knew him. He said he stood it for about five days then flew back to Miami where he ran up to the first man he saw when he got off the plane, pleading, "Would you please take my autograph?"

Since Jack's death we share the box with Walter Matthau. The autograph problems are the same. He too is a wonderful companion, much more knowledgeable about the game. He generally ambles in about the third inning with a brown paper bag of sandwiches which he shares with those around him. He is no fashion plate. I once said to him, "What are the odds of a man who looks like you becoming a movie star and remaining one for so long?" He responded seriously, "The odds are so great that they are incalculable." I believe him. He knows a great deal about odds and betting and has the losses to prove it.

Most of the time, however, we have sat in the rarefied atmosphere of the O'Malley box where, along with the game, we get fine company, drinks, and a wonderful dinner.

We baseball fans are a voluble lot, but Walter O'Malley's wife, Kay, was an overwhelming exception. I never heard her speak. She was born with a normal voice. While she was in college her larynx was removed because of cancer. That took place over fifty years ago, and one can only wish that present-day recoveries could be so complete. She and Walter were married for forty-seven years. I have not known happier couples.

To watch them converse was a wonderful experience, inclined the first few times to make the eyes mist a bit. Her lips moved, her expressive blue eyes reflecting her mood. His casual lip-reading was incredible. He, of course, answered normally. After a while one totally forgot that no words came from her mouth. Being her friend for over twenty years was without question the greatest dividend baseball has ever given me.

The day Dodger Stadium opened I took my officemate, the late William Goetz, whose art collection recently was auctioned for eighty-five million dollars, to the game. The O'Malleys hosted an early buffet lunch. Not wanting Bill to be taken aback by Kay's condition, I told him about it beforehand. As we walked to our seats later I said to him, "What did you think of her, Billy?" Bill, a cynic possessed of a black sense of humor, responded, "It's the greatest way to keep a marriage going that I've ever seen. I'm going to mention it to my wife tonight, but she'll never go for it." It was a cover-up, however. It was easy to see that he was impressed with her, and he was not easily impressed.

She conversed with her children and other family members just as fluently. It was a large family. Kay felt she was the mother of the Dodgers and everyone in the organization felt the same way. An untold number of ballplayers, coaches, and front-office people learned to lip-read out of respect and affection for her. Vince Scully is to this day a perfect lip-reader. With the aid of his binoculars he can pass along at will comments made on the field—laundered comments.

Kay made very few concessions to her condition. She would have a pad and pencil handy, but expected to use it a minimum. Such high hopes generally brought out the best in people, but some, including myself, never did get the hang of it. During countless games she would converse with me as though neither of us were aware of my proven obtuseness. Eventually I would be forced to say, "Kay, write it down." She would do it, but invariably would rap my knuckles with her pencil and say, "Try harder."

The Koufax-Drysdale era of the early sixties was certainly the highlight of Walter O'Malley's career. These two great pitchers, now Hall of Fame members, carried their light-hitting teammates to a treasure trove of division championships, pennants, and World Series victories. Two-to-one and three-to-two victories prevailed. There were many stories about the Dodgers' absence of run production. One had it that Don Drysdale was flown ahead of the team to get a good night's sleep before pitching the opening game of a road trip. On landing he was told that Koufax had pitched a two-hitter. He immediately inquired, "Did we win?" These games were fingernail-biters. Our spirits rose and fell between our splendid pitching and weak hitting. One evening in Walter O'Malley's box I said to him, "When I die I want to be cremated and have my ashes spread over second base at Dodger Stadium where so many men have died before me." Dodger-mania was rampant. I attended games constantly and at dinner parties carried a portable radio, to the annoyance of hostesses.

Highlights of this remarkable era were Dodger-Yankee World Series classics circa 1963. We traveled to New York for every game, always meeting Kay and Walter afterward. The rooting level was intense. At one of the home games some raucous Yankee fans right behind us were constantly yelling at Koufax comments like "Break your arm, you bum" and "You have no guts." My wife, Harriet, noticed that my fuse was getting dangerously short. She turned to the hecklers and said sweetly, "Please, fellows, have a heart. Sandy is my brother." They apologized abjectly and told her that he was "the greatest ever." There was never another word from them. I was delighted to inform Sandy that he had a new sister, and the usually reserved Koufax enjoyed it hugely.

The era came to an end, as all things do. In 1979 we lost both Kay and Walter. I will miss them always. Peter, already President of the organization and thoroughly trained by his father, succeeded him as Chairman. His style is completely different from Walter's, but he is an equally fine executive. Fortunately, Peter and his attractive Copenhagen-born wife, Annette, "adopted" us and we never missed a beat in the owner's box. *The Guinness Book of Records* can certainly state with impunity that Annette has attended more Dodger baseball games than any other Danish citizen in history.

I knew I would always be a fan, but was certain that my greatest baseball moments were behind me. I was wrong. The game has a happy way of surprising its supporters. The 1988 miracle Dodgers, picked to finish near the bottom of their division, shocked the baseball world by winning it. Conventional wisdom, including mine, was that this was a happy aberration but that Dodger Blue would be no match for New York's mighty Mets. The Mets were soundly thrashed and most of the New York sportswriters are still trying to figure it out. In an uncharacteristic burst of modesty, Dodger manager Tommy Lasorda said, "We beat the best team in the National League."

The newly minted National League champions were described as "the weakest team to ever reach the World Series" and certainly no match for the American League sluggers from Oakland. To the surprise of everyone except the team, they routed Oakland to become world champions. The storybook quality of the 1988 season stands tall above all my earlier baseball thrills. The team did poorly in 1989 and not much better in 1990, but there is always next year.

I look forward to the season with the same excitement that I did seventy years ago. How many interests last that long? Damn few.

# ME

*and*

# MY DOUBLE LIFE

I GRADUATED FROM the University of Chicago in 1935, having transferred from Dartmouth after my sophomore year. My grandfather, Julius Rosenwald, had been a major contributor to the university, and my family thought that my enrollment there would be a meaningful symbolic gesture. I enjoyed the university, but I was by no means a dedicated student. In fact, it was touch and go as to whether or not I would graduate. President Robert M. Hutchins told me later that he had heaved a sigh of relief when I "passed" out of that institution.

America at that time was just coming out of the Great Depression, and jobs were hard to find. It must be said in all honesty that I had no firsthand knowledge of this monumental American trauma, and the fact that employment was scarce rather pleased me. I had only the vaguest idea of the true meaning of a job and certainly was no exponent of the work ethic.

To my regret, I experienced no difficulty at all getting situated. My family met in my absence and decided that investment banking was my forte. Although we lived in New York then, I was informed that I was to go to work in Chicago for A. G. Becker & Company, an outstanding firm with longtime ties to my grandfather and to Sears, Roebuck, of which he had been chairman of the board. I was mildly surprised to learn of my aptitude for the investment business since a C was the best grade I had ever received in any math course. I did not, of course, disagree; rebellion was not in fashion at the time and I realized that I had to do *something*.

After a pleasant summer in Europe, I took the 20th Century Limited to Chicago to set forth on what I vaguely supposed would be my lifework. My sole preparation had been to reserve a suite at the Ambassador West Hotel.

★　　★　　★

The great day arrived with sudden and rather alarming inevitability. Outwardly calm, I ate the breakfast I had ordered from room service and then took a taxi from the cab rank on Goethe Street to a corner one block from the office of my about-to-be employer, which was at 120 South La Salle Street. I walked that last block briskly, trying to convey an impression of purpose.

I reported to the man whose name I had been given. In those days there were no forms to be filled out, and I was simply taken around to the back and introduced to the head messenger. In less than three minutes my career was underway.

The messenger room was of modest size and, to put it mildly, austerely furnished. Along one plain white wall were a desk and chair for the head messenger, and on the opposite wall a long bench for the rest of us. Having met my new colleagues, I was seated at one end of the bench. Within moments the head messenger called "Next," and the young man at the other end of the bench got up, received a packet of securities, and left to deliver them. We all moved up a notch and my place was taken moments later by a returning messenger. Business was brisk and I was soon in the head slot, ready for my first assignment. As luck would have it, I was given some securities to deliver to Laurence Stern & Company; since I had known Laurence Stern all my life, I felt up to the task.

Those were gentle days indeed! None of us were bonded, and we strolled innocently around La Salle Street with packets containing hundreds of thousands of dollars' worth of securities.

Upon delivery of my packet, I was given a receipt and returned with a new confidence to my place at the end of the line. Gone were my well-hidden feelings of inadequacy and my doubts about my sketchy mathematical background. This seemed to me to be invigorating work with an easily defined purpose. I felt certain that I would do well and that I would enjoy it, particularly when the weather was pleasant. Chatting with the other messengers was easy, aimless, and impersonal. At eleven-thirty the all-powerful head messenger told me to go to lunch. "But," he said, "there is no need for you to eat in a restaurant every day. You can simply bring your lunch and save the money." I told him I was pleased to hear this, though I had misgivings about how it could be accomplished.

At the end of my first day, I walked a block away and took a cab back to the Ambassador West Hotel. I called the maître d' of what was the precursor to the Pump Room. "Look," I said to him, "I have to take my lunch to work. When my breakfast is sent up, send along something I can take with me. It's very important to me." He promised to take good care of me. He certainly did.

With my breakfast the next morning was a wicker picnic hamper containing roast chicken, hard-boiled eggs, a thermos of hot coffee, salt and pepper, half a dozen paper napkins, and some grapes—more than enough to feed all the messengers. "For Christ's sake," I complained to the waiter, "I can't take this to work." The thought of taking part of it seemed too much to cope with since time was of the essence. Already hardened to quick executive decisions, I gave the hamper to the waiter for his family's dinner.

At work I was asked why I was not brown-bagging it. I replied truthfully that I lived alone and that bringing my lunch was impractical.

Occasionally my messengerly duties varied. One day I was told to report to Mr. Becker's secretary. Jimmy Becker was a friend of my family's and had, of course, been in on the arrangements involving my training and future career. Needless to say, however, I did not see him during business hours. I made my way through to the front of the house and Jimmy's secretary pointed to two suitcases. She told me that Mr. Becker was going to take the 20th Century Limited to New York. My assignment was to check his suitcases at the La Salle Street Station and take the checks back to her. Since it was raining, she gave me money for carfare. The suitcases were quite heavy. I took a cab both ways and returned with commendable speed. As I gave the secretary the checks, Jimmy, smoking a pipe, walked through on his way to his office. He glanced my way with some surprise. I saw him that weekend at the club, but neither of us referred to our brief encounter.

Within an amazingly few days, my goal became crystal clear

to me. It was not success that I craved but anonymity. I realized fully that the simple, pleasant, casual friendship of the messenger room would surely evaporate if the full scope of the difference between my lifestyle and that of my associates were ever brought into the open. I was truly leading a double life. A kind of Cinderella in reverse, I got going around midnight. The town was gay and fun, filled with attractive girls, friends, and parties. The Chez Paree was in full swing and so was the late great Ernest Byfield, the owner and nonpareil host of the Ambassador Hotel and the Sherman House.

Many of the stars of the entertainment world played Chicago. All of them stopped off between the Century and the Super Chief and headed like lemmings for the Ambassador Hotel. Ernie Byfield, overwhelmingly amusing and looking like a satyr, was the hub of this unceasing activity. He had been a great friend of my late father and, though I was considerably younger than most of the regulars, I was tolerated. Certainly I was the only messenger at A. G. Becker who drank and dined with the likes of Gertrude Lawrence, Jack Buchanan, and Spencer Tracy. Whenever I was asked about my occupation, I said I was an investment banker, and nobody cared enough to pin me down as to my exact function. I took great precautions not to be accidentally photographed with these people, whose pictures appeared regularly in Chicago newspapers. Beyond a feeling of fatigue most mornings, which was assuaged by brisk, regular walks, I found that having a job was not at all bad.

Approximately six weeks later I was upgraded, leaving the happy confines of the messenger room for the bond cage. Here things took on additional complexity. My mentor was a somberly dressed gentleman named Mr. Mitchell. He was truly accommodating and expressed regret that he never had time to explain to me adequately the very real intricacies of the cage. Actually, he deluged me with instructions. Despite the soothing quality of his voice, which, after a late night, cut my powers of concentration to almost zero, I learned. First of all, I found out where the securities that were delivered to the messenger room came from. Secondly, the advantages of working on commission rather than on salary became clear to me, and I acted immediately. My method was simple, direct, and, in all modesty, effective. I merely telephoned the head of our family office in New York and inquired as to whether we did any business with A. G. Becker & Company. When he replied in the affirmative, I suggested politely that he credit those transactions to me; then I got word to the proper authority that I would be happy to work on commission. My salary jumped in one week from $18 to $327, certainly an indication that my family had not been wrong in singling out this field of endeavor for me.

For the most part, none of the moves from one department to another bothered me very much, though I was happy to leave the bond cage. Standing there all day, after some of my nights, was not a particular blessing.

I did find the trading room difficult. The traders were so rushed that they were forced to assume I could absorb the details of their profession by osmosis. This was a totally false assumption, since they conducted business entirely over the phone in phrases completely foreign to me. When they left their chairs, they moved swiftly and sometimes one of them would trip over me.

I began to take long lunch hours and to make occasional visits to the horse parlors that were then very much a part of the life of Chicago. (These emporiums were brilliantly described in the film *The Sting*.) I have never been a racing fan, but I enjoyed placing my bet and, after being given a complimentary drink, hearing the call of the race from a distant track delivered by a man in a cage, I could well afford gambling since my commissions continued to flow.

By this time in my training, the Chicago winter had come and gone. An announcement appeared on the bulletin board that tryouts for the A. G. Becker baseball team would be held a few evenings later. In this area I did not suffer at all from lack of confidence and, indeed, made the team easily. We played other La Salle Street houses after work in Lincoln Park, and I developed a lot of college spirit for good old A. G. Becker.

My enjoyment, however, ended—literally in a flash. Although it happened more than fifty years ago, the event that unmasked me is brilliantly engraved forever in my mind.

It was a lovely early evening. The spectators were limited to a few employees loyal to A. G. Becker and the other firm. I was at bat. Suddenly, as if in a bad dream, a photographer appeared along the first-base line. He knelt and snapped my picture. I was dumbfounded. When I asked him the reason he said, "Aren't you Julius Rosenwald's grandson?" I said that I was, and he replied that that was the reason. I struck out.

Speechless and crestfallen, I returned to our bench. I had never lied, but I had desperately wanted to be like all the others. One of my teammates, a messenger, turned and said to me, "Don't feel bad. We knew it all along."

As I sat on that bench, a basic lesson of life was dramatically driven home to me: Leading a double life is difficult at best and almost always doomed to failure.

Time, of course, lessened the impact of the blow, and not long afterward I was transferred to A. G. Becker's New York office.

Looking back, I don't think I made much of a contribution to A. G. Becker. I can say, however, that I was a distinct asset to the baseball team.

# ME

*and*

# MY LIFE AS
# AN USHER

FROM THE BEGINNINGS of motion pictures until the mid-1930s, the technique indicating the passage of time was a series of dissolves showing the audience the changing of the seasons. Leaves falling from the trees in the autumn, snow on the ground in the winter, the blossoming buddings of spring and the lushness of summer were the staple. The great German-born film director Ernst Lubitsch broke that mold in a variety of ways. In one film the viewer saw the attractive legs of the leading lady walking down Park Avenue with a short dachshund on a leash. At the next dissolve the dachshund was a little longer. In the following one noticeably longer. The final dissolve showed him at full length. Presto! Time had passed.

I was a very short dachshund, age twenty-eight, when I first served as an usher on July 8th, 1941. My swan song, barring a miracle, came thirty-four years later. I was by then in my sixties, a full-length dachshund getting a bit smooth in the tooth. I have quite a collection of cuff links and silver pens, all happy reminders of stops along the way. However, the first and the last, together with the most amusing, have served as a rite of passage, weaving together important fabrics of my life.

The morning of July 8th, 1941, dawned cool and pleasant in New York, an omen that the day would not be marred by the heat or rain that often plagues outdoor events at that season. The groom, Orvil Dryfoos, chose to spend his last bachelor hours with me. We had become friends during our prep school years. By the time we finished college we were so close that he had a room of his own at our family summer home at Croton-on-Hudson. Adored by my mother, he came and went as he pleased. He was a regular at poolside lunches, usually accompanied by an attractive girl. Indefatigable at tennis and swimming, he was such a handsome, cheery addition that if he had other plans his presence was sorely missed. He plugged along uncomplainingly at his prosaic stockbroker job, doing well enough in a mediocre environment. Orv, I thought pleasantly, was quite a catch.

It was to Croton that we headed for a final bachelor swim and lunch before driving over to Hillandale, the beautiful White Plains estate where the ceremony would take place. The bride, Marian Sulzberger, was the lovely daughter of Arthur Hays Sulzberger, publisher of the *New York Times,* and the extraordinary Iphigene Sulzberger, daughter of the newspaper's founder-publisher. Marian and Orv were very much in love. It was idyllic. She too, to put it mildly, was quite a catch.

Little of this crossed our minds as the ceremony drew closer. Both devout baseball fans, we felt that the timing of the wedding, which collided directly with the All Star baseball game, was unfortunate. We listened intently to the radio as we drove to White Plains. When we arrived at Hillandale the game was tied. I joined the groom to listen in an upstairs bedroom where he changed. I was already suited up.

Lord knows the bridal party was prepared. We had rehearsed enough to put on the Ziegfeld Follies. We had marched endlessly down the aisle and back, first indoors, then in the great outdoors of Hillandale. The time came for the ushers to report for duty to escort the wedding guests to their seats. I lingered at the radio until the father of the bride burst into the room, commanding me to do my duty. I bolted, leaving Orv, who had some ten minutes of waiting time, to hear the game.

As the bridal party started down the aisle, our one and only performance, it was clear that the rehearsals had paid off. The Radio City Rockettes could not have outdone us. I walked directly past my friend to my allocated position as he waited for his bride. A moment later, radiant and lovely, she came down the aisle to the traditional music on the arm of her father. The beauty of the day and the setting were magical. The world, as I saw it at that moment, was innocent and peaceful. There was not a cloud in the sky. I was happy.

As we marched out I again passed the newly minted groom,

who chose that moment to speak his first words as a married man. "Lazzeri tripled in the ninth," he said to me softly but clearly. It was crystal clear the New York Yankee second baseman had made a key hit, enabling the American League to win the game.

I had once asked Orv if he expected to go to work for the *New York Times*. Genuinely surprised, he said he could not see that happening. He had not reckoned on the awesome dynastic will of his new mother-in-law, the paper's controlling stockholder. Functioning quietly behind the scenes, she was for well over a half century the spirit and conscience of the *New York Times*. She did not interfere with day-to-day management, but on vital policy matters hers was the clarion voice. Less than six months later, Orv waved goodbye to Wall Street to join the staff of America's newspaper of record.

The imminence of U.S. participation in World War II quickly pushed into the background my memory of that day when the American League beat the National League in the ninth inning of the All Star game. Orv drew an extremely low number and was among the first to be summoned by his board. I received a telephone call from him moments after his physical examination. "They told me," he reported, "that I have a bad heart. I will never be drafted."

His seemingly fine physical condition, high energy level, and exuberant good health elicited a natural response from me. "These Army doctors are all third-raters. Make an appointment with your own doctor. I'll meet you there." Even in the waiting room I was not particularly nervous. He reappeared in an amazingly short time. All Army doctors, I learned, are not third-raters. This diagnosis was right on the nose. Even if the enemy took Colorado, Orv would never be called up. The only happy part was that there was no dire prediction. He was simply ordered to be cautious and moderate.

His lifestyle changed. He had played his last set of tennis. He walked to and from his office. He watched his diet. He looked exactly the same. Gradually, as time passed, the worry about him lessened and was forgotten.

For twenty years he held increasingly important posts at the *Times,* handling them all with grace and ability. It would have been understandable, had he become so totally immersed in this fascinating world, that our friendship suffered. It never happened. Each time I went to New York I lunched with the top editors and their guest of the day, who constituted a panoply of the world leadership. He absorbed the basic Sulzberger tenet like a sponge: Possession of total power makes the need to use it rare.

Marian's parents were friends of my parents. Over time I grew to know them well. Arthur was soft-spoken, surefooted, and gifted with the ability to rule his domain lightly but firmly. When asked how to become the publisher of the *New York Times,* he invariably replied, "Work hard and marry the boss's daughter." Iphigene, always Mrs. Sulzberger to me, ranks high on any list of America's great matriarchs. She died at ninety-seven years of age, having lived to see her father, her husband, her son-in-law, and her son publish this family enterprise. She lived through wars, crises, good times and bad, always using her low-profile control only when necessary.

Hers was a life of understated elegance. She must have found the final decade a disappointment and a puzzlement. The city that she loved so much was taken over by people who worshiped at a far different shrine. Ostentation, glitz, press agents, and the highest possible profile, all repugnant to her, were the order of the day.

On a trip to New York in 1946, Arthur Sulzberger invited me to lunch alone with him. I was flattered but puzzled, particularly when he told me he wanted my advice. He proposed to send the *New York Times* by plane to Los Angeles to be delivered to subscribers by messenger. He felt strongly that the *Los Angeles Times* of that era was not serving a potential readership that would welcome the new cross-continent arrival. What did I think?

I was enthusiastic, but asked if it would not be extremely costly for the subscribers and the *New York Times.* He agreed that his newspaper would lose money on it. Before too long, he predicted, a new age of electronics would change everything in the media. He cheerfully proclaimed this move a whim and a primitive marketing test. It would take two hundred subscribers to trigger the experiment. "How," he asked, "would you feel about trying to round them up?"

Together with a friend, I had the list within a week after my return. Contrary to my prediction, no one balked at the price. Orv and Marian flew out for the first issue. They were our houseguests at a party when the first copy was delivered.

Arthur had not bargained on the hardball that the *Los Angeles Times* would play. Stung by Arthur's feeling that Los Angeles was the most vulnerable large city for his experiment, they successfully prevailed on all their large advertisers to steer clear of the invader. After a relatively short test, the bloodletting was too high. The experiment ground to a halt. It has always seemed to me that the *Los Angeles Times,* almost overnight, became a far better newspaper.

In 1961 Arthur, still in quite good health, decided on semi-retirement. He wanted to round off his career by acting as adviser to the new publisher. Orv had been with the *Times* since 1942. He had handled with distinction every assignment given him. The Sulzberger choice was not difficult. My close and longtime friend became the publisher of the *New York Times.* The odds on this happening at the time of our graduation from college are incalculable enough to make the winning of a lottery ticket almost a sure bet.

In 1979 a remarkable biography, *From Iphigene,* written by a granddaughter, was published for "family and friends, but not for general publication." In it she said she loved Orv like a son. "We shared a common love for the outdoors and on long walks through the woods at Hillandale we would talk about business and politics." She recalls "how his eyes would twinkle under his bushy eyebrows and a broad smile would light up his handsome face."

That same year, 1961, was marked by a bitter printers' union strike against the *Times* and seven other New York dailies. Mrs. Sulzberger recalls that when conciliation seemed impossible and negotiations on the verge of collapse, Orv would step in and persuade the negotiators to resume their talks.

When the strike finally ended, Orv and Marian went to Puerto Rico for a much-needed vacation. A few days later he had a heart attack. He was flown immediately to New York, but on May 15th, age fifty, he died. Mrs. Sulzberger wrote that "there is little doubt that the unrelenting tension of the long strike had cost him his life." I do not like to disagree with her, but at the moment we left his doctor's office I would have happily settled for an additional twenty-two years. The strike undoubtedly provided a cruel push.

The eulogy was delivered by the *New York Times* columnist James "Scotty" Reston. He said in part, "The death of Orvil Dryfoos was blamed on 'heart failure,' but that obviously could not have been the reason. Orvil Dryfoos' heart never failed him or anybody else, no matter what the doctors say, they cannot blame his heart."

Orv's loss created a void in my life that will never be filled. From the start the loss was lessened by the bonds forged over the years of his marriage to Marian. We became closer than ever. Harriet and I saw her regularly on every trip to New York. We telephoned. We corresponded. Threads so securely tied do not become unraveled.

The Sulzbergers had thought that Orv would be publisher until his retirement age. By then their own son, Arthur Ochs Sulzberger, known to one and all as Punch, would take over. He was only thirty-seven years old when his brother-in-law died. Without hesitation, Punch was named publisher.

For many years I had thought that Punch had been a ring bearer at the wedding. Only recently, we talked about it. He denied this vigorously, stating that he was an usher. "The youngest," he said, "but definitely an usher." I asked him if there had not been considerable talk about his being the ring bearer. He agreed, but said that he had prevailed. He has indeed. From the start he proved himself an outstanding publisher. Thirty years have passed under his able leadership.

In 1965 Harriet received an enigmatic telephone call from Marian, asking if we were planning a trip east in the near future. When she heard that there were no such plans afoot she asked if we would fly in. It would be impossible for her to be coy, but it must be said that she was not forthcoming. We flew in. That evening Marian picked us up to go to an apartment in the Tudor City section where we met Andrew Heiskell, the six-foot-five-inch Chairman of Time, Inc.

We had cocktails, but still nothing was mentioned about the reason for all of this, although it was unnecessary to seek out an astrologer. Finally I could stand it no more. "What," I asked, "is this all about? Have we come here to bestow our blessing or what?" Andrew said he thought Marian had explained everything. She said she felt shy. I told them that for two sophisticated people they had handled the matter extremely awkwardly, but that we were delighted for the opportunity to inspect Andrew. Hugs, kisses, and handshakes were exchanged. We went on to a very gay dinner at which Andrew and I consumed several bottles of excellent red wine.

There were no ushers at that wedding. It was at the Sulzberger New York apartment and very small indeed. Arthur was in a wheelchair.

Our friendship has successfully overcome the three-thousand-mile geographic chasm in a variety of ways. For eight years Andrew was Chairman of the President's Committee on the Arts and the Humanities. I was Vice Chairman. He demanded that we conduct our business not as volunteers, but as though we were being handsomely paid. As a result, we accomplished much.

The bond that started between Orv and me remains a strong one after the passage of more than a half century. I find myself in total agreement with what Scotty Reston said about his heart.

In 1955 I received a phone call from my close and somewhat eccentric friend, Collier Young. Collier was, at that moment in time, married to Ida Lupino, a fiery, attractive star of her day and also a friend of mine. Collier was a rather slight, nice-looking, sandy-haired man of medium height. He was the product of an impeccable family and had an education to match. He was attracted to Hollywood early on. As a writer and as a producer he fared well and survived in the jungle of his choice. He was, above all, a glittering link to the end of the F. Scott Fitzgerald era.

White flannels were as congenial to him as are overalls to a factory worker. George Gershwin was perhaps put on earth to write the music that expressed Collier. He smoked a great deal. He drank a great deal. In those days there was not the onus on these twin sins that exists today. Collier was regarded as a hail-fellow-well-met, a splendid drinker who was sometimes in his cups. In addition to Ida Lupino, he had been married to Joan Fontaine. He was mockingly reconciled to his supporting role, adjusting to his reflected fame with wry good humor.

I thought that long ago I had reached the stage that no call from Collier would surprise me. I had underestimated him.

"Congratulations, my boy, you are about to be an usher at a wedding." I said mildly, "You're already married, Collier, and this country does not look favorably on bigamy." "Not for me, not my marriage," he said kindly, "You are going to be an usher at the wedding of Milo Frank and Sally Forrest."

I barely knew the bridal couple. Sally was Ida's protégée. Milo, as I recall, was a minor agent at the William Morris agency. Not unreasonably, I questioned Collier as to why I was chosen to be usher for people I really did not know. "Well," he said, "the answer is very simple. Ida and I are choosing the bridal party." I asked Collier if he did not think it would be appropriate if the young couple chose a bridal party made up of their friends. "Not at all, not at all," said Collier. "This whole thing will be much better if we pick everybody. Trust me on this one, this is going to be a first-class event at our house, and their friends will not tone the thing up at all." He went on to give me the date and tell me that striped trousers and a morning coat would be the uniform of the day.

I shared many fabulous times with him. A single party we attended captured the quintessential Collier Young. The host was the late beloved Harry Kurnitz, writer, art collector, wit, and bon vivant. Harry lived in a lovely house high above the Chateau Marmont, overhanging the Sunset Strip and the city below. His guests were a composite of much that was glittering and attractive about Hollywood.

Arriving alone, I was one of the last to leave, making my way a trifle unsteadily to my snappy beige Chrysler convertible. I started the ignition, put the gear in reverse, and stepped gently on the gas. The motor roared but nothing else happened. After repeating this procedure several times, I surveyed the situation and saw that my front wheels were firmly embedded in a rut. As I stood, uncertain as to what to do, Collier, considerably the worse for wear, appeared. "What," he inquired loudly, "seems to be the matter here?" I described the problem briefly. As he often did at such times, Collier sprang into instant and, in this case, disastrous, action. "We've had enough drinks for ten men," he pronounced. "One good strong push should get things moving."

He was, regrettably, right. A single mighty shove freed the car from its moorings. Instantly it developed a mind of its own. Instead of stopping, as we had every right to think it would, it drifted imperceptibly left and started down the incline of the driveway. Collier and I stood transfixed as the car, gathering speed rapidly, began down the steep descent from Kurnitz's mountain aerie. For long moments it remained glued to the right lane, making the curves as though driven by an invisible Barney Oldfield. Suddenly, suicide bent, my beloved Chrysler executed a ninety-degree right turn and plunged over the abyss. It crashed wildly below us, a scant hundred yards from a house filled with sleeping people. A slight miscalculation by the driverless car would have wiped out everybody in that house. From the crash the car made on landing, it was obvious that it could not be picked up by a blotter. Collier and I sobered up as if by magic. I stood immobilized and numb. Collier, however, was brisk and helpful as ever. "You will want to tell the local constabulary about this," he said. "As for me, I will never help you with anything else as long as I live." With a jaunty wave of his hand he got into his car and was gone. This was the entrepreneur of the Forrest-Frank nuptials.

I went to the MGM wardrobe department for my morning coat and striped trousers. They outfitted me handsomely on the first crack. We had several pleasant wedding rehearsals. I cannot remember the name of the other ushers and bridesmaids. I do recall clearly that I was the least famous. Ida was gracious and determined. Collier acted as though we were a battalion about to go under siege, urging us to stay calm and be firm. During this time I grew to know slightly the bride and groom. They could not have been more pleasant. They adjusted to being pawns at their own wedding, taking it in good part because Ida really cared for the bride and Milo was swept up in the vitality of these events as propelled by Collier.

The day of the wedding inevitably arrived and the bridal party appeared on cue through a great wooded glen at Ida and Collier's lovely home, where around the pool and with a distinguished audience on view, the knot was tied. Before we got under way, Collier, our leader, kept turning to us and admonishing us in a loud tone not to panic, assuring us that all was going well and that we should keep our eye on the ball. No one, that I could observe, was on the verge of panicking, only amused by the show that Collier was putting on. The wedding went off without a hitch. The bride was radiant. Ida was a beautiful matron of honor.

The supper that followed was pleasant, marred a bit by the fact that by the time Collier made his rather long and breezy toast he was definitely three sheets to the wind. On my way home from the wedding, I was vastly amused by the entire happening. Another typical Collier Young adventure.

Quite naturally, I did not keep up with Sally and Milo, although I received from them the obligatory cuff links. To the best of my knowledge they have remained married, which is more than can be said for some of the weddings at which I lent my dignity as an usher, including that of Ida and Collier, who were divorced not long after this.

The wedding had an enormously healthful effect on my life. When I returned the morning suit to the wardrobe department I said to the head of it, "This is a great, great outfit." He replied, "It should be, it was worn by Spencer Tracy in *Father of the Bride*." I was deeply shocked. Tracy was a very portly fellow. I made it a point to take a good look at him within the next forty-eight hours and it only validated my feelings. The fact that his clothes fit me without alteration came as a real blow. I vowed to take off twenty pounds. Every time I came close to wavering, the picture of Spencer Tracy came to my mind and I remained steadfast. I took the weight off and never put it back. I should call Sally and Milo one of these days and thank them for having me as an usher.

One of my first telephone calls in 1975 was from Robert F. Wagner, New York City's three-time Mayor, inviting me to be an usher at his January 30th marriage to Bennett Cerf's widow, Phyllis. I knew about their plans to marry and was enormously pleased about it. Phyllis has always been a constant in my life and I had known Bob for many years.

Harriet had definitely been cast in the role of Cupid, in which she was a total success. Phyllis waited a long time after her loss before, rather hesitantly, beginning to accept invitations from friends. Sometime later we were in New York and insisted that she fly with us to Washington to attend a party given by our close friend Nancy Dickerson. On the plane back to New York the next day Phyllis confided to Harriet that Bob had been calling her to go out to dinner. She said she was at a loss as to what to do. Harriet was not at a loss for one moment. She said firmly, "I'll tell you what to do. Invite him to a small dinner at your home. We are good friends of Bob's and we'll stay over for it. Let's see what happens. We'll take it one step at a time." Phyllis was insecure, but Harriet pushed her. One step at a time proved to be the proper road map since the next step was to the altar.

The wedding took place in a lovely, smallish church, St. Thomas More's at 89th Street and Madison Avenue, before a distinguished group that jammed the pews. There, these two started their marriage and I, barring a miracle, concluded my career as an usher.

It was a joyous one for me. I was, in point of fact, spending more time than I cared to think about as a pallbearer. I had played that sad role at Bennett's funeral, which created a unique juxtaposition of events in my life that jogged many memories.

The world had spun around countless times with me on board during the thirty-four years since I first served as a member of a wedding party. The innocent joy I felt on that occasion was denied me but was replaced by deeper, equally satisfying emotions. Then I only looked forward. In my sixties, I could not help but look back. The rearview mirror provided a pleasurable view.

The bride and groom had both loved and admired my mother, whose leadership in many causes, particularly the plight of the city's neglected children, made her a leading, beloved citizen of New York. She had a group of younger women whom she called "her girls." When a crisis arose she would bring them together at her apartment, outline the problems and the keys to a possible solution. Each of them received her assignment to be accomplished by the next meeting. Since they adored her, they fought like lions and enjoyed many successes. Phyllis was one of "her girls" and attributes her leadership role in civic life to that early training.

My mother crossed swords with Bob Wagner often, complaining bitterly to the Mayor about various things on which she felt the city was derelict, particularly with regard to the care of children. When I lost my mother in 1960, Bob joined Governor Nelson Rockefeller and Mrs. Franklin Roosevelt, who flew back from Europe to be present as speakers at her Memorial Service. Bob said in part, "I know oftentimes we would meet on some of the problems in which she was interested. She felt that I didn't move fast enough or did not find enough money, but she kept up the battle and in so many areas she won a great victory, not for herself but for the city, and particularly for the youngsters who needed her help and her leadership."

Nobody gets elected Mayor of New York three times without having a rare combination of qualities. He has them. He has always been a political animal, the middle man of a formidable New York dynasty. His father was the famous Senator Robert F. Wagner. One of his sons was president of the City's Board of Education. He loves both his sons and reveres the memory of his father. Hardly a day goes by that he does not mention him.

To this day, walking down Fifth Avenue with Bob is like being in the Easter parade. Taxi drivers honk their horns and yell hello to him. People walking in the opposite direction greet him with an affectionate smile, remembering gentler days in the life of the city. His response is always the same. "How are you? Good to see you. How have you been?" His memory of names and background of enormous numbers of people is awesome. "Trick of the trade," he says dismissively. Like Robert Redford, Bob is a Natural. The Wagner family is of German descent, but to see him walk blissfully in endless St. Patrick's Day parades, Jewish Veterans Day parades, or Italian Columbus Day parades, always liberally toasting the celebrants, causes people to identify him only as the quintessential New Yorker.

It is all part of a pattern that he could not break if he wanted
to.

The four of us were once in Barbados at the home of Claudette Colbert. Nestled some two thousand miles from the tip
of New York City, it hardly has borough status. Everything
was marvelous, including the food. His Honor and I determined to take a long walk on the beach every morning before
breakfast as a tiny gesture to combat our caloric intake. Every
time we passed people going the other way, Bob slowed down
to a crawl saying, "How are you? Good to see you." It finally
irked me. I said, "Bob, you are not walking. You're campaigning. Most of these people are not Americans, let alone
New Yorkers. Besides, you're not running for office." He
apologized and our pace quickened notably. Thirty steps later
a couple passed us. The man said in a very Bronx accent, "How
are you, Mayor? We're a long way from home, aren't we?"
Like a flash, Bob turned on me. "That's two votes you've cost
me and we haven't even had breakfast yet."

Bob, suspicious by nature of teetotalers, has on tap a series
of toasts to offer when the spirit moves him, as it often does.
They are repetitious and pleasing to his friends.

On a beautiful day at the pool he observes, "Let's have one
more against the inclement weather." An all-purpose regular
is, "Shall we have one more in the spirit of good fellowship?"
For slightly more ceremonial occasions peopled by senior citizens, he raises his glass and intones, "There are very few of
us left to which the good Lord says Amen."

He is an extremely loyal Yale man, particularly to the class
of '33, which must have been the largest to ever graduate. Even
today he meets or refers to a class member on an almost weekly
basis.

In college he invariably migrated to New York on Friday,
partook of the pleasures of the city, and caught the Sunday
milk train back to New Haven. He had his timing down perfectly, always reaching his room in time for the Senator's Sunday call from Washington. His answer was like a Victrola
record. "Gee, Dad, I'm glad you caught me. I was just on my
way to the library." He would then sack out for the rest of
the day.

Bob's public service was far from over at the conclusion of

his three terms. He later served with distinction as the United States Ambassador to Spain, which he describes as far more dignified than worrying about the Sanitation Department's problems.

As a cap to his splendid career, Bob and Phyllis went in 1978 to Rome, where he served as President Carter's Envoy to the Vatican. They both enjoyed this experience hugely. When the Reagan administration came into office they paved the way for an extremely smooth transition for his successor, Ambassador William Wilson. The Wilsons were most appreciative and a close friendship was forged. Bob goes through life keeping friends and building friendships.

Last year I attended Bob's eightieth birthday celebration in New York. It speaks eloquently for the affection and esteem in which he is held. Only a few months earlier New York University renamed their School of Public Service the Robert F. Wagner School of Public Service, an event which thrilled him mightily. Now, on his birthday, the first awards of the newly named school were presented to four of our closest friends, President and Mrs. Ronald Reagan and Ambassador and Mrs. Walter Annenberg. Rock-ribbed Republicans all, they were proud to accept an award named in honor of this lifelong Democrat.

Phyllis and Bob are the people we see first and most often on trips to New York. Service as an usher has been kind to me. If my career is indeed ended, I went out on a high note. It may be that I am not washed up yet. I admit I am in no position to wait another thirty-four years. On the other hand, I have indicated a willingness to participate on behalf of virtual strangers. I will just have to sweat it out.

Tragically, on February 14, 1991, Bob died. Flags were ordered flown at half-staff for thirty days as memories of the contributions of the beloved three-time Mayor surfaced. The crowded services at St. Patrick's Cathedral were befittingly warm. I flew from Los Angeles and once again sadly assumed the role of honorary pallbearer. There is no need to change any words about Bob in this book to the past tense. I will never think of him that way.

# ME,
# JOE LOUIS,
## *and*
# THE CHAMPION'S FINEST THREE MINUTES

I HAVE HAD in my lifetime the extraordinary good fortune to observe at close hand a man perform, at high risk, a totally unique act of great generosity and courage. It was done with grace, skill, and modesty in the glare of unceasing public scrutiny. It took place fifty years ago, and I will always treasure the memory.

At the end of my Wall Street stint in 1940 I landed a job almost immediately as advertising agency representative on the Rudy Vallee radio program, a big entertainment factor in those pre-TV days. I loved my work and New York was an exciting place to be. I was truly shocked when it suddenly ground to a halt in the form of a card ordering me to report for active duty to 90 Church Street, headquarters of the Third Naval District. I had totally forgotten that I was an inactive member of the Naval Reserve. America was at peace. The war seemed far away. Unwillingly and ungraciously, I reported, took a physical, and was assigned to Public Relations.

My first phone call, after several days of inactivity, was an eye-opener. I was to report to the Commandant. I wondered nervously what I could have done so wrong so quickly. I was not out of uniform; I had no uniforms.

Rear Admiral Adolphus Andrews, on the other hand, cut a commanding figure in his handsome gold-braided uniform. Asking me to be seated, he plunged right in. "Navy Relief," he told me, "is in sorry shape." I had never heard of Navy Relief, but shook my head sadly. "The Port of New York is a busy place," he said, "and we are finding a lot of sailors, wives, and sweethearts stranded here. They all turn to Navy Relief. Our peacetime budget won't do it. We need, and damn quickly, a fund-raising event that raises a great deal of money for Navy Relief. I know you've had a lot of experience."

My record showed that I was a director of a charitable foundation. I tried desperately to explain to him the vast difference between making charitable contributions and raising large sums of money for charity. "You'll do fine," he said in dismissal. "Call on me for any help. Good luck." I returned to my desk, which I now regarded as a way station to the brig. The week finally dragged to an end.

Friday nights for me meant fight night at the old Madison Square Garden. There were plenty of good fighters, and attendance was not limited to championship bouts. A group of us had regular tickets and had dinner at the Garden Club. Ruling this roost was the Garden promoter, Mike Jacobs, known to all as Uncle Mike, who also controlled the destinies of the great heavyweight champion Joe Louis. He was a lean, bald man whose poorly fitting false teeth were a source of glee to all. Making his rounds at the various tables, he sat with us while I was ruefully explaining my new liaison with Navy Relief.

Jacobs immediately expressed interest. "That might be something for the champ," he said. "Drop in and see me Monday morning." Our meeting was short and overwhelmingly productive. Mike told me that he had talked to Joe Louis at his Detroit home over the weekend. The champion would fight in the Garden on January 9th, 1942, and donate his entire purse to Navy Relief. Mike would contribute his share. "We'll charge thirty dollars for ringside seats," he said. "Navy Relief should make a bundle." I agreed wholeheartedly. In today's terms he was asking two hundred dollars for a ticket that normally sold for five or six dollars.

What I knew of the fight game impelled me to question my benefactor. "Who," I asked timidly, "will he fight?" If Mike sensed my reservation he did not show it. The champion would fight Buddy Baer. No need to say more. The two had fought the year before in Washington, D.C., Louis winning on a disqualification in the eighth round. The younger brother of former heavyweight champion Max Baer had been no pushover for Louis, knocking him through the ropes in the first round. It took me a moment to digest the fact that Louis could conceivably lose the heavyweight championship of the world without receiving a dime.

I reported this happening to Admiral Andrews in record time, thinking he would regard this jackpot as the norm. He was enormously excited, however, jumping to his feet, shaking my hand, and telling me warmly that my assignment was "to stay on top of this matter at all times." A Navy car and driver would be assigned to me. I felt that I had just returned from a successful visit to Lourdes.

Announcement of the title fight was made from Admiral Andrews' office on November 13th, 1941. Nationwide headlines trumpeted that the champion would contribute his purse, Jacobs would serve without fee, and Baer would receive a minimum amount. There would be no complimentary tickets. The public, in the first throes of a patriotic fervor unmatched since that time, reacted with excitement and admiration. On Sunday, December 7th, the Japanese attacked Pearl Harbor. President Roosevelt proclaimed it "A date which will live in infamy." America was at war. The lives of all citizens were affected and it magnified the patriotic contribution of the champion.

Three days later Buddy Baer arrived from Sacramento, California, to set up training camp at Lakewood, New Jersey. He was met at Penn Station by a group of midshipmen, naval officers, and a Coast Guard band. Outgoing and huge, he told the large press turnout that he weighed two hundred fifty-five but would train down to two hundred forty-five for the bout. His abilities would never match those of the Brown Bomber. However, it was apparent that anyone who took a full blow from this friendly giant would be lucky to survive it.

On December 19th the champion arrived from Detroit at Grand Central Station. The crush was so great that even from my vantage point I could barely see him. He walked forward slowly, eyes slightly down, as New York's finest cleared a path for him. After seeing Baer, the champion looked like a light heavyweight.

He was whisked off to Mike Jacobs' Garden office, where I met him. The stillness of his body created an aura of quiet power. His handshake was surprisingly light. I said simply, "This is a fine thing you are doing." His stolid face lit up with a warm smile and he said gently, "It's a good cause."

At noon Joe went to the State Athletic Commission Office.

After greeting Baer and formally signing contracts for the press, he was off to the quiet of Greenwood Lake. Thirty-five miles from New York, nestled in Ramapo Hills, this little town had excellent training facilities and was a Louis favorite. I, ever faithful to duty, went there early on and was so fascinated that I never got to Baer's camp.

The press corps, Joe's large retinue, fans, and hangers-on gravitated daily to the site. The Bomber skipped rope, hit the light and heavy punching bags, and boxed with his sparring partners under a merciless microscope. Only the grueling early-morning roadwork was private. His manager and trainer met daily with the press to answer questions on his progress, weight, and mental outlook. These repetitious sessions provided the material for the unceasing publicity spread daily across the country.

The inevitable victims of the training camp were his four sparring partners. They were the key to the champion's preparation. Normally they went only one round each day, but one was enough. They were usually knocked down and always shaken. The champion was often referred to as Shufflin' Joe. His legs carried him relentlessly to territory where his fists could do their work with lightning speed. His eyes were fascinating; his feet shuffled but his eyes stalked.

One afternoon I was informed that the champ had invited me for dinner. I accepted and enjoyed it so much that I became a virtual regular. Here one saw a different Joe. Sitting relaxed at the head of the training table, he smiled and laughed a lot, enjoying the trade talk and banter. I stood out like an extraordinarily sore thumb in my Navy uniform and was the target of some good-natured barbs from the head of the table.

One night Joe asked me if I wanted to sleep over and run with him early the next morning. December jogging in the hills of Upstate New York was no day at the beach, and I declined with enough alacrity to earn some appreciative chuckles from all hands. His next invitation was to punch the light bag with him. I would have enjoyed trying this but the thought of that huge, restless press corps scared me off. His final offer was to go one round with him "real light." That one I did not deign to answer. I merely looked at him as though he were a candidate for a padded cell. Amid the general laughter he closed the topic very deftly. "You're smart not to get in the ring with me," he said. "You're the one that worked out my share of the purse against Baer."

The ticket sale opened in New York City with great fanfare on December 22nd. Benefits today follow one on top of another and are sold by highly organized, pressurized committees. Navy Relief had a Benefit Committee, but it was not really needed. The action was at the box office and the ticket brokers and there was plenty of it.

On December 23rd the Brown Bomber put in one of the most strenuous days of his training career. In addition to his customary roadwork, he sparred five hard rounds and topped it off with ten rounds of floor work. He was rounding into form and did not want the Christmas day off to affect him. Defending his title without benefit of fee was obviously very much on his mind.

Meanwhile the challenger was training well. Reports from his camp were upbeat and contributed to the fight buildup. There were a few anxious moments on December 24th, when Baer was involved in a traffic accident, but he escaped virtually unscathed and missed only two days of training.

On Christmas Day Louis shared a turkey dinner with his retinue and the neighborhood children. It is not the happiest time to be in training camp, but he was cheered by a thousand telegrams, letters, and cards commending him and wishing him well.

After Christmas the pace quickened. On the last day of the year Louis was examined by Dr. William H. Walker of the State Athletic Commission. Pronouncing him in tiptop shape and more than ready to go fifteen rounds, Dr. Walker told the press, "Louis exhibits fewer physical changes over the years than any fighter I have ever examined." His assessment was factual. He did not profess to read the tea leaves of the future. The physical changes were to come later, at first gradual, then fast and tragically unforgiving.

On January 3rd I watched Joe's workout with awe as he savagely stopped two sparring partners. The *New York Times* writer reported that he "flashed the form that made for dis-

tinction among heavyweights even before he gained the title."
Trainer John Roxborough told the press he would like to see
Joe enter the ring against Baer "as sharp, accurate, and vicious
as he is right now."

Both fighters broke camp on January 6th to return to a truly
excited New York City. Baer was reported to be in fine shape
and ready for the fight of his life. During this period Louis had
received his Army draft notice and obviously faced a major
interruption of his golden years of earning power.

On the morning of the fight a famous sports columnist wrote
that Louis "now moves into a class by himself in heavyweight
history, putting his title on the line and not taking a cent." He
commented that perhaps the champion had lost a trifle of the
speed with which he had blasted his way to greatness. He had,
after all, defended his title twenty times.

The great night found the Garden bedecked with American
flags to welcome the sellout crowd of twenty thousand. The
working press extended back to the fourteenth row. The preliminary matches finally ground to a conclusion. The crowd
grew quiet. The challenger was the first to come down the
long aisle and enter the ring, receiving polite applause. From
my excellent, and paid-for, thirty-dollar ringside seat Baer
looked like a dreadnought weighing, as he predicted, two
hundred forty-five pounds. Joe was conceding five inches in
height, ten inches in reach, and forty-eight pounds in weight.

A cheer rose from those in a position to see the champion
start his walk to the ring. It grew in volume as more of the
crowd saw him, and he entered the ring to the greatest ovation
ever accorded a fighter. It cascaded and roared down on him
as he stood impassively in his corner. It took a long time for
the ring announcer and the clanging of the bell to get a sem-
blance of quiet.

It must have had an effect on Baer. Fighting for a fraction
of the challenger's usual share of the purse, he found himself
cast in the role of potential spoiler. Louis later said he felt that
he had twenty thousand people in his corner. The introduction
of champions, former champions, and celebrities seemed endless. A moved and silent audience stood for the National An-
them. The fighters met in the center of the ring for their

instructions. As for me, I was suddenly lightheaded and could feel my heart pounding. Gone was my amused pride at being the catalyst for this truly unprecedented happening, and I did not give a tinker's damn about the newfound riches of the Navy Relief Society.

The fact was that over the past weeks I had grown very fond of Joe Louis. More important, I had come to understand that he was a pawn in all of this. Powerful and famous, but nevertheless a pawn. Others had arranged the fight and still others would benefit from it. He and he alone stood at risk. "Don't let him lose," I prayed. "Don't have him go into the Army next week stripped of his title." The bell clanged.

Joe finished his challenger in two minutes and fifty-eight seconds of the first round, pounding him to the canvas twice for nine counts before that. He fought with a ferocity and concentration he had not shown for a long time. Baer proved his courage, twice rising gamely, but the Brown Bomber, savage and alert, never gave him a second to regroup. A deadly right-hand punch was the finisher.

Baer had no reason to be ashamed. The Bomber had, on occasion when he was fired up, done this before. In June of 1938 I had seen him demolish Max Schmeling, a darling of Nazi Germany and a far better fighter than Baer, in one round at Yankee Stadium.

I made my way to the champion's crowded dressing room. He told reporters that he had been very eager to end the fight. He said he had never punched harder and that Baer was game to get up. He said he was proud to fight for Navy Relief and would do it again for the Army. I caught his eye in all the chaos. He raised his arms in the victory pose and gave me a warm grin. I left the Garden exhilarated by my friend's prowess, but feeling more than a little like Cinderella at the stroke of midnight.

The next day's newspapers were dominated by every aspect of the fight. One writer said Joe had run out of opponents and could be defeated only by Father Time. Another said he would be justified in giving up his title to enjoy the fruits of his labor, having long since put away enough money to live out his life in luxury. Counting other people's money is usually an exercise in rosy optimism. That certainly proved tragically true in his case.

Three days later I rode from Madison Square Garden with Joe and Mike and watched them present Admiral Andrews with a check for $89,000, the equivalent of $670,000 in today's currency. Jacobs said he wished it had been $100,000 more and Louis expansively wished it had been a million. I walked with them to their car. Joe was off the next day to be inducted at Fort Monmouth. We shook hands briefly. I never had the good fortune to meet him again.

Four years later he was discharged from the Army. During the next two years he defended his title four times before retiring. That long an absence from the rigors of training camp and fighting was like a century at his age. Physical examinations showed no reason not to ply his trade and he needed the money. I wish that he had fought in the Pay TV era. I have thought of him so often after seeing fighters not worthy of carrying his mouthpiece lose lackluster fights and go home with purses undreamed of in his day. Thirty-five rounds of boxing were involved. Sixteen of them were against Jersey Joe Walcott, forty-eight minutes of brutal savagery against a hungry opponent able to give the Bomber all he could handle. He kept his title but it was a tragic final chapter to his monumental career.

Father Time, as predicted, finally met him toe-to-toe and overwhelmed him, reducing his health and his existence to a shambles. He had absorbed too many punches and, lacking formal education and responsible financial advisers, he could not fight back. He became a greeter in Las Vegas and later was confined to a wheelchair. When death came to him in 1981 he doubtless welcomed it.

His 1979 biographer, Rugio Vitale, properly portrayed him as a man replete with faults and virtues. My path, however, crossed his at the exact zenith of his life, which started so humbly and scaled such heights. I knew him as a champion and a gentleman.

# ME

*and*

# THE FRANK SINATRA COMPOUND

MILLIONS OF PEOPLE can remember the first time they ever heard Frank Sinatra sing. I am one of them. The year was 1942. Frank had just left the Tommy Dorsey band. He was playing for the first time at New York's Paramount Theatre, the engagement that launched him into orbit. The tabloids featured nothing else, so when my friend Bob Weitman, manager of the Paramount Theatre, invited me over to see him I quickly accepted. Bob's office featured a glass window overlooking the stage with the sound piped in.

Frank played eight shows a day, so I did not have long to wait before the reed-thin figure walked onto the stage. The squealing yells from the famous bobby-soxers reverberated through Bob's office. It was a new sound, a screaming expression of adulation and curiously innocent eroticism. They were, Bob told me sadly, almost impossible to dislodge, fiercely fighting all eviction efforts and drastically cutting the grosses.

Frank, a big band behind him, began to sing. He never got through more than a few bars without being drowned out by his audience. It was immediately apparent that he was destined to be more than the flavor of the month, although no one could foresee the magnitude and longevity of the career that was starting to unfold.

Bob took me backstage. Frank and I exchanged the first handshake of a friendship that has lasted over half a century. I mentioned that I was having a party the following Saturday night and wrote down my address. It was a bedlam, but he nodded and thanked me. To my surprise he showed up, his clothes torn a bit by the bobby-soxers as he made his mad dash to the car. This scene has been a constant during his career, although he quickly acquired enough protection so that no one could lay a glove on him. He knew no one when he came in, but quickly became the focus of the evening. There was always plenty of ad lib entertainment. When asked to sing he politely declined, although possible accompanists included Richard Rodgers and Frank Loesser, saying that he had sung enough for one day. I believe it was the first party of its kind that he ever attended.

I wax a bit maudlin about those evenings, which went on for some years with various group members alternating as hosts. They were completely informal. Sandwiches and drinks were served in the early morning. Lindsay and Crouse, authors of *Life with Father* and other hit shows, mediocre but eager entertainers who sometimes wrote special material for us, were regulars. So was John Steinbeck, a quiet teddy bear of a man. Ethel Merman sang and sang. It was far from a closed club. Other show business people invariably drifted in. I initially gained admittance under the sponsorship of my longtime friend Frank Loesser, whose unique talents were cut short far too early. They were, in retrospect, the happiest party evenings of my life.

Nineteen ninety was, in the words of a Sinatra standard, "a very good year." In May he played three concerts at Radio City Music Hall, less than ten blocks and more than fifty years from the time I first saw him at the Paramount. The concerts were sold out within hours of the tickets going on sale. Scalpers did a land-office business. Many bobby-soxers, now in their seventies, were in the audience. So were their children and, to his great satisfaction, their grandchildren. An amazing percentage of the cheering crowd that gave Frank standing ovations were in their twenties and even younger. It is the ultimate test of the longevity of a career that has seldom strayed far from the top. And better things were yet to come in December, on his seventy-fifth birthday.

There have almost always been names that for a time have ranked ahead of his in the field of personal appearances, but for the half century since he struck out on his own no one can rival his consistency. The number of composers, lyricists, arrangers, orchestra leaders, sidemen, recording people that have passed through his life defies calculation.

From the beginning one could see the qualities that years

later inspired the song "My Way." He was willing to risk a job, a contract, or a major career setback that often seemed reckless. About music matters he had great convictions and about other matters he was prepared to back his hunches to the hilt.

In every city there is a music station that devotes a great amount of time to Frank's recordings. A Philadelphia disc jockey plays only Sinatra songs and, since there are over four hundred and fifty to choose from, he is easily able to avoid repetition.

His singing the songs of great writers such as Berlin, Rodgers, Hammerstein, Mercer, Cahn and other landmark names is a firm bridge between what was popular in the yesteryear and what is popular today. America is gripped by a strong nostalgic yearning, and the music that Frank has recorded is beginning to enjoy a renaissance.

Frank's singing has always appeared effortless. Into it have, of course, been poured endless hours of rehearsal, plus great discipline and a respect for the material he sings. He credits this to Tommy Dorsey. He has also poured an unbelievable amount of liquor into his throat and vocal cords from which his blessings flow. His throat has been much kinder to Frank than he has to it. He once went to see a new doctor who asked him if he drank. Frank allowed that he did. The doctor next inquired as to his average daily consumption, to which Frank responded modestly, "I have thirty-six drinks a day." The doctor said he was serious. Frank replied that he was equally serious. He patiently explained that he drank a bottle of Jack Daniel's every day, and that broke down to thirty-six drinks. The horrified doctor asked Frank how he felt in the morning, to which the Italian street singer, so dubbed by his friend Harry Kurnitz, replied, "I don't know. I'm never up in the morning and I'm not sure you're the doctor for me." The doctor, Frank reports sadly, died soon after the consultation. The Jack Daniel's distillery has acknowledged Frank's loyalty by deeding him an acre of their land in perpetuity. Jack Daniel's has long given way to vodka. Frank has cut down some, but there was after all plenty of leeway. He says pridefully that his throat and vocal cords should be in a bottle at Harvard.

Frank has not always been a model of decorum. As he says,

"The New Jersey roadhouses where I started singing were not owned by the Vanderbilts and the Rockefellers." This facet of his personality has been vastly overplayed, due in large measure to the fact that his relations with the press over the years have varied from hostile to aggressively hostile.

Kitty Kelley, author of *His Way,* holds the unenviable title of America's mistress of the scurrilous book. Not many writers have the stomach for this genre. Ms. Kelley, an indefatigable, painstaking researcher, has the patience and experience to amass vast amounts of material. The result is a book that, after a fine-tooth-combing by a battery of attorneys, is a non-suable model of half-truths, quarter-truths and innuendos.

I have found him, as have many others, an impeccable, caring friend. Certainly he has brought into my life a variety of marvelous experiences, the most indelible of which encompassed a decade of Christmas holidays at his home in Palm Springs. We were first invited in 1962 and accepted instantly. We had been there often enough to know that we were certain to have a fine time. An insatiable name-dropper, I constantly let our holiday plans be known. It had the results that all name-droppers crave: people were impressed.

Frank was not put on earth to be an exemplar of serenity, but he has always been at his easiest when his Palm Springs gates closed behind him.

We were, it turned out, a group of fourteen. The dictionary description of tradition is "something passed on by custom." This strikes me as a flexible definition requiring perhaps one hundred years of maturation in England, fifty in Maine, and five in Southern California. None of us had the remotest idea that first year that we would double my arbitrary Southern California benchmark.

The first welcoming sight on entering the compound is a warm, beautifully lit Christmas tree. It would be natural to think of it as part of the season. Not so. It is lit day and night three hundred sixty-five days a year. "Every day is Christmas for me," Frank explains. "I was poor long enough to learn that."

The main house features a snug, comfortable living room adjoining the frequently used bar. Next comes a study with a passage leading to an attractive dining room. Beyond that is an enormous state-of-the-art kitchen equipped to turn out food on a constant, steady basis. Stepping outside the living room, one sees a semicircle of guest cottages with a pool, an expansive deck, and tennis court. Off to the right is the Great Hall, a large projection/game room and bar.

Most of us were friends at the outset, and Frank's easy, warm hospitality made us closer. The guest list and accommodations never changed. As the holiday house parties accumulated, our time together became increasingly meaningful.

We shared the first cottage with Bennett and Phyllis Cerf. Bennett was a founder of Random House and a star panelist of the popular TV program *What's My Line?* I've known the usual complement of people in my life, more than most, but the only one I ever really envied was Bennett. He had two jobs that he loved so much he would have done either one for nothing. Phyllis was a top Random House editor of many books, including the famous "Dr. Seuss" series. She remains one of the closest friends of my life.

Next came a smaller cottage housing Pamela and Leland Hayward, probably the most fascinating couple in the compound. Leland was a Hollywood film agent and Broadway producer extraordinaire. English-born Pamela Hayward, now the widow of Averell Harriman, is without question the Sinatra compound's greatest success story. Married to Winston Churchill's son Randolph, she spent the World War II years as a resident at 10 Downing Street. Pamela has the gift of making every man she talks to feel enormously important. In the decade between divorcing Randolph and moving to New York, her lovers included Elie de Rothschild, Gianni Agnelli, Prince Aly Khan, Stavros Niarchos, Aristotle Onassis, Averell Harriman, and Edward R. Murrow. Asked by Bennett one afternoon by the pool if that was pretty much the entire list, she replied sunnily, "Perhaps, if one does not count ensigns and second lieutenants."

One afternoon a group of us were sitting around the Jacuzzi dangling our feet in the hot water. Suddenly Pamela stood up, removed her terrycloth robe and, without the benefit of a bathing suit, stepped into the Jacuzzi. I, for one, was aghast.

My behavior was a classic example of misplaced loyalty. Jumping to my feet, I ran into our cottage to alert Bennett of the great happening. He was beside himself with anticipation, but by the time he had changed his glasses, stumbled around, and shuffled out to the Jacuzzi, Pamela was sitting with the others in her robe. Bennett begged her to have another go at it, but to no avail.

In marrying Leland, Pamela went directly counter to the dictum of her friend Mrs. Loel Guinness, whose first commandment was not to defy the gods by marrying a man who was not wealthy. Leland had the financial ups and downs that went with his chosen territory.

She was a superb wife to Leland, who later on became the victim of a long, terminal illness. Before too long she recouped by marrying Averell Harriman, this time living by the Gloria Guinness rule book. She made the last years of his life wonderful and, as has been said, has found it far better to be the widow Harriman than the widow Hayward. She presently lives a rich, full life in Washington, where she is the doyenne of the Democratic Party.

Leland is accurately described by Pamela's predecessor, Slim Keith, in her posthumous autobiography as exotic, eccentric, and charming. She tells in detail of her desolation when Pamela plucked him away from her. He was indeed a spontaneous, mischievous delight.

Since he was a crack photographer, I mentioned to him one day that I might like to make it a hobby. He told me with boundless enthusiasm that I was entering into a wonderful world that would prove an endless joy. A lesson or two might have been the logical starting point, since he had enough equipment to open a small shop. He insisted that we set forth for Palm Springs to purchase what he called beginner's equipment. I thought he meant something only slightly more advanced than a Kodak. I returned the stunned owner of several thousand dollars' worth of cameras, lights, and lenses that I could barely distinguish from his own. He immediately set everything up for some easy, beginner's shots of cacti and blooming flowers and told me to look into the finder. I expected to see the splendor which lay immediately ahead. Instead, when Leland asked me what I saw, I truthfully replied that I saw only the reflection of my own eye. Leland, horrified, made an on-the-spot judgment that I had a built-in disability for photography. He urged me never to try it again and said that in any event he could not waste time with more lessons. I was on my own, dependent upon the thick, incomprehensible manual. It was a typical sardonic Hayward ploy. Properly embellished, it made the rounds of the compound to the joy of everyone but me.

Opposite the main house, anchoring the compound, was a larger building that was the holiday home for three couples.

First came Rosalind Russell and her husband, Freddie Brisson. It was an unspoken fact that all of us, certainly including Frank, regarded Rosalind as the first among equals. Some years later Frank decided that he wanted to end his performing career. He was bored with all of it. The sum total of the effort, thought, and rehearsal that goes into a personal appearance or a recording session had become only drudgery. The standing ovations which he had heard so often were no longer a reward. He gave what he truly thought was his final performance in Los Angeles. Afterward, a small cavalcade of cars drove to Rosalind's home for drinks and to share with Frank what he honestly believed to be the end of his epic. It was an extraordinary moment in his life. He chose to ride alone with Rosalind.

She was, of course, a durable, magnetic star in the movies and on the stage. More importantly, being with her, sharing her laugh, her humor, and joyous, dynamic spirit lifted the heart. She accepted completely the good and the bad that makes up life. She has been gone fifteen years. To this day when I think of her, which is often, I feel a stabbing pain. I recall vividly Jimmy Stewart's eloquent tribute to her which ended, "Take care of her, God. We've sent you our very best."

Down the way were domiciled Mr. and Mrs. Jack Pressman, she better known as Claudette Colbert. Years have passed since, with a modest raising of her skirt and a saucy French look, she hitched a much-needed ride in *It Happened One Night,* something her costar Clark Gable could not manage.

She is the principal beneficiary of Ponce de Leon's heralded discovery of the Fountain of Youth. Long inured to compliments, she attributes it all to high cheekbones. If all the women in the world with high cheekbones looked like Claudette, what a blessing it would be. Today, in her eighties, people often say that she is looking better than ever.

Beneath her vivacity and infectious laugh is a very French commonsense quality. She has an amazing knowledge of who she is and feels no need to tinker with her signature hairdo or to be center stage. A presence like hers often feels threatening to other women. Not so with Claudette, whose life is filled with caring friends. She had much to do with the very texture of our times together during that Sinatra decade.

William and Edith Goetz lived in the final suite. He made many films, including *Sayonara,* and headed production at 20th Century–Fox and Universal Studios. After his retirement from the motion picture business he and I shared offices for twelve years. We were close friends. He was enormously popular; people were constantly amused by his hard-nosed, sometimes cruel wit. He was a great adapter to life, a quality he had reason to put to daily use.

I have always felt that Norma Desmond, brilliantly played in *Sunset Boulevard* by Gloria Swanson, was Edie Goetz's biographer. She was born the daughter of Louis B. Mayer, king of kings in the pioneer motion picture firmament, and carefully raised to be a Hollywood princess. Like many royals, she adored her career, worked hard at it, and for a long time she enjoyed huge success.

The Goetz dinner parties were the number-one invitation in the town. The house was lovely and beautifully furnished, the appointments perfection, and a Cordon Bleu chef. The crown jewel was the Goetzes' superb collection of Impressionist and Post-Impressionist art that a few years ago went under the hammer for eighty-eight million dollars. Dinner guest regulars included Clark Gable, Tyrone Power, Jimmy Stewart, David Niven, Frank Sinatra, Danny Kaye, Rosalind Russell, Claudette Colbert, Loretta Young, and a small contingent of top executives.

Edith was overthrown in midcareer, an occupational hazard for royalty. New picture-makers and new stars took over. A less tenacious person would have recognized the inevitable, but she was a fighter. Never for one instant did she consider herself to be even in temporary exile. However, the unceasing battle took its toll. During our Sinatra years she was, with great effort, treading water. Billy's popularity and charm had masked much of her Machiavellian character, but after his death in 1969 it was all downhill. By the time her own life ended she had alienated both of her daughters and almost all of her friends. I have always felt that her greatest contribution to our compound life was the fact that she often slept through lunch.

Next came the cottage of Arthur and Leonora Hornblow. An extremely popular couple, invited everywhere, it was natural that they were on Frank's list. A gourmet and a dandy, Arthur was the producer of over forty films during his long Hollywood career, including *Hold Back the Dawn, The Major and the Minor, Cass Timberlane, Oklahoma!,* and *Witness for the Prosecution.* He left Hollywood at the top because both of them found the lure of New York irresistible. He lived there happily the rest of his life.

Leonora has, more than anyone I know, a gift for friendship. She told me at lunch recently that she is paying a price that she never anticipated. "Hardly a week goes by," she said, "that I don't get a telephone call from an author asking me for an interview on a biography being written about a close friend. They are time-consuming and I hate them."

I had no choice but to admit that I had asked her to lunch to get her insight on Bennett Cerf for my book. We roared with laughter. The rest of the lunch was spent reminiscing about Bennett. She helped me enormously. I do not see the requests for interviews diminishing.

We were blessed with two incomparable bachelors, Harry Kurnitz and Yul Brynner. Harry's rheumy eyes viewed the world through thick glasses. He was tall and had dreadful posture. He was, from the very start, frail. A Don Juan lived within him but it was not visible externally. Harry arrived in Hollywood in 1938. He wrote some forty films, several prosperous Broadway comedies, and what he described as "a thin but unimpressive collection of novels." His writing varied from very workmanlike to very good.

What made his reputation, first in Hollywood and then in the capital cities of the free world, was not his writing but his wit and lifestyle. Commuting between America and Europe, he became known in all sorts of high-flown circles as a legendary wit, a title he richly deserved. A random sampling comes to mind.

A reporter once asked him what it was like to live as a screenwriter during this Golden Age of Hollywood. He responded, "The general sensation is like sinking slowly into a giant vat of warm farina."

On one occasion he had just finished writing a Broadway play. The press agent wrote him for some background material. He responded, "I am presently in Africa as an indentured slave to Howard Hawks, who for some reason has chosen this locale for what I think will be a Western. I play dreadful golf, gamble too much, can see nothing without my glasses, and am constantly on the prowl for a girl that looks exactly like Audrey Hepburn and loves only me."

I once lived with him for a year; it was one of the happiest experiences of my life. He practiced the violin constantly and played it terribly. When I occasionally complained he said, "I am used to having listeners slap the wrist of my bow hand. If you did that it might have a salubrious effect." He occasionally gave evening musicales featuring a trio of Gregor Piatigorsky on the cello, Arthur Rubinstein at the piano, and Harry at the violin. Except for a rare grimace, the cellist and the pianist gave no indication that the violinist lacked concert ability. They stood a pace behind him when taking their bows.

At one time his paper matchbooks had on the cover a typewriter with a pair of hands poised over it and underneath the legend, "These are our only tools."

Once when a lady apologized for spilling a little wine on his sleeve he replied gallantly, "Not to worry. This suit has had so much wine spilled on it that I never send it to the cleaners. I simply have peasants in to trample on it."

People sought and clawed to get him for lunch, for dinner, as a houseguest, anything at all just to be with him. He had a room of his own in Loel Guinness' beautiful home in Normandy. One morning Guinness, suffused with affection for Harry, said, "Would you be more comfortable if I built you your own house on this property and have someone take care of it for you?" Kurnitz replied, "You're obviously eager to get me out of this house. What have I done to offend you?"

For a number of years Harriet and I stayed in Paris at the Georges V Hotel, not our favorite, because Harry was living next door at the Georges V apartments. It was our custom to have dinner with him on our first night. On one occasion we received a note telling us to meet him at Monsignor, a restaurant famous for its arsenal of violins. On arriving at our table we were instantly surrounded by an embarrassing concentration of fiddlers performing only for us. They played until Harry, deep in their midst, turned over his violin to one of them and sat down at the table.

His endearing façade masked a lonely man. The ladies adored his company, but for the most part he went home alone. He was at heart a romantic, but he did indeed search for an Audrey Hepburn replica. It simply was not in the cards. He traveled from place to place with his typewriter and the music he loved to hear. In the end, it was his huge, loving army of friends that were his family.

My most vivid memory of Yul is his speaking from his grave to television viewers. The enigmatic face, the shaven head, the piercing eyes, and the unique voice urging us not to smoke and gently informing us that he would be on the planet today had he followed his own advice. He was a dead man as he spoke, knowing the act itself would follow soon and be welcomed.

Yul, more often than not, thought of himself as the King of Siam. Plucked from the obscurity of a CBS TV director into the lead in the Rodgers and Hammerstein masterpiece, he became an overnight, highly recognizable star. He made many films, some outstanding. He played other stage roles, but that opening night marked the coronation of a new monarch. Over the years he took it on the road endlessly and revived it on Broadway. It was his life and his livelihood, although he would say ruefully that he had been put on earth to enrich Richard Rodgers and Oscar Hammerstein and later their estates.

He lived in grand style, more appropriate to a real king than a pretender to the throne. To see the paganlike luxury of his dressing rooms and hotel suites, whether he was settling in for a week or three months, gave one an instant understanding of him.

At the Sinatra compound his façade vanished. He emerged with the full complement of virtues and frailties, making no attempt to hide behind a role. He was easy, pleasant, and extremely eager to be well liked. He dressed as the other men did, although his physique and bearing made the rest of us look slovenly. It was rather like being with Douglas Fairbanks, Jr., in a dinner jacket. He makes everyone else look as though they were wearing hand-me-downs.

Occasionally, sitting cross-legged on the floor in a Gypsy outfit, he would play the mandolin and sing mournful Gypsy songs. He was vague about his birthplace and forebears, but almost certainly first saw the light of day somewhere in the vast stretches of Outer Mongolia. He played dreadful golf. One day, however, he shocked his foursome by hitting a bunker shot worthy of Jack Nicklaus within two feet of the cup. When complimented he replied nonchalantly, "Why not? I was born in a sand trap."

Long after our Sinatra decade ended I received a letter from him describing in detail how, in the belated Swiss spring, he had used his putter to clear snow and ice between his ball and the cup. He followed this, he wrote proudly, by snaking in a thirty-foot putt. I could see it all as clearly as though I had been present. I immediately wrote him that he had always used his putter like a rake and that the putt was probably fifteen feet at the most. I received from him a three-word cable: "Closer to twelve." The King of Siam did indeed smoke strong cigarettes and long, expensive cigars. Regrettably, he paid the ultimate price.

Frank ran his bachelor home superbly. Our days were pleasant, easy, and formless. Everything one wanted was at the ready. Tee-off times were arranged. Cars were at our disposal. A tennis pro was no farther away than the telephone. An informal buffet lunch was served every day at the pool, although any kind of breakfast was available for late sleepers. This, of course, included our host, who certainly was not an early riser by any stretch of the imagination. Sitting around the pool, and occasionally getting into it, was unquestionably our major activity. In those days we were happily unaware of the damage inflicted by the sun.

At the cocktail hour the tempo changed. Frank was the motor for that; he gave these nightly gatherings a party atmosphere. To put it mildly, the cocktail hour was unhurried. The flower-filled dining room, with excellent red and white wines on the tables, had a festive air. Italian dishes were a staple. Frank, a truly fine pasta chef, often spent much of the late afternoon preparing a specialty for us. More often than not, the ladies found gifts at their places. Sometimes for variety we dined in a private room at one of the local restaurants. The dinners were always ordered ahead and prepared with loving care since all of the restaurateurs were hoping to get a call from Frank.

Then it was on to see a double feature in the Great Hall. Prominently displayed was a dart board featuring ghastly likenesses of Hedda Hopper, Dorothy Kilgallen, and Louella Parsons, permitting Frank to keep his distaste for columnists green and verdant. The films ended around midnight. The houseguests were definitely getting sleepy. By Frank's body clock it was nine P.M. at the latest. In his formative working years his job ended at two A.M. and lasting sleep habits were formed. These were his hours of relaxation from a pressure-cooker life of making gold albums, wildly successful appearances, and some excellent films under an unceasing public scrutiny. On top of that, he was a world-class insomniac. Frank was ready for some serious drinking and conversation, interspersed with telephone calls to friends around the world, most of whom he awakened. As many of his songs have poignantly reminded us, midnight is not the hour to be alone, and Frank had no intention of getting caught in that spot.

The fact that we were annually invited back was proof positive that we were satisfactory guests. Bedtime, however, was our Achilles' heel. The ladies drifted out quietly one by one. By one-thirty we were a sleepy, potentially mutinous crew with a resolute host who kept an eagle eye on all the exits. Bennett, ever the pragmatist, came up with the solution. We would rotate. Two of us each night would stay the distance. It was not perfect but it worked well enough. Life, after all, is a series of accommodations. Although never admitting it, I actually grew to enjoy my Sinatra sittings replete with rich, well-told show-business reminiscences. As I walked to our cottage at dawn's first light I developed a faint hope that the Jack Daniel's distillery would deed me some land. It never happened.

Once each holiday we would fly to Las Vegas via a chartered transcontinental jet festooned with balloons, flowers, and a full complement of flight attendants plying us with drinks and hors d'oeuvres. Limousines took us to the Sands Hotel, Frank's Las Vegas home. The gambling capital with its familiar Strip was foreign to many of us. Our host was the reigning Emperor. He embodied the glitz and glitter of the town. When he played at the Sands, the overflow filled the other hotels and casinos. Getting a table at a Sinatra performance was like sitting on the fifty-yard line at the Super Bowl.

We entered the hotel escorted by security worthy of a summit meeting, Rosalind, Claudette, and Yul making up a strong supporting cast as we made our way through the casino and into the first show. The hotels vied for top entertainment. The Sands competed successfully.

Following the show we enjoyed a lavish dinner in a private dining room with a delegation of subservient hotel executives at the ready. Then it was on to another hotel for the late show, after which we piled back to the Sands for gambling. Each of the ladies was presented with a bag of chips. They were all mild gamblers at best and usually cashed in most of the chips before we left for the return flight to Palm Springs, making them several hundred dollars richer than when they arrived. Not many players could make that claim.

On our return, usually around four A.M., we went into the Great Hall for an early breakfast. Frank was in his element since it was one of two nights during our annual stay that he did not have to argue with his guests about the appropriate time to retire. For most of us on the Las Vegas evenings it was lights out by four-thirty, but Harry and Yul often stayed to enjoy a few extra drinks with Frank, enabling him to go to bed at his favorite hour, seven A.M.

We were not at all blasé about New Year's Eve. For most

of Frank's life this had been a work night and he relished being a host. Much has been written about the despondency and despair of people who are lonely and alone as the year changes. We, like thousands of other groups throughout America, were seeing the New Year in with old friends and had much to be grateful about. It was an event to savor.

A Lucullian dinner was served at nine o'clock in the gaily festooned Great Hall. Close friends were invited and these were coveted invitations. Afterward tables were cleared away and a wonderful orchestra took over. Other guests joined us and by the time "Auld Lang Syne" was played we were fifty or sixty strong with others pouring in as the night progressed. We were blessed with wonderful entertainers who performed, and Frank, not a party singer by choice, never failed us. No one had to draw straws to sit up with him. We were all on Sinatra time. When we did finally fold our tents we could see early golfers on the adjacent course starting another frustrating year.

One New Year's Eve Frank told us he had an offer he could not resist. He was going to sing in Chicago to "make a little bread." Everything was laid on as though he had been there and, with the time change and his private plane, he strolled in around two-thirty announcing that he had "a little black boy who would sing for us." That was Sammy Davis, Jr. Frank meant nothing pejorative; the friendship between the two men spoke for itself. It was impossible for Sammy to do anything but go flat-out. He gave us an electrifying show and Frank yelled up to him, "They're getting more here than they got in Chicago." When Sammy died I thought wistfully of that night so long ago when he held us enthralled.

Our decade finally drifted away, as all good things do. We lost Harry Kurnitz and Bill Goetz. It seemed better to quit while we were so far ahead.

On December 12th, 1990, Frank celebrated his seventy-fifth birthday in concert at the Brendan Byrne Arena in East Rutherford, New Jersey, not far from his birthplace. The New York Times, in a long, glowing piece headlined, "Sinatra's Voices in the Passage of Time," stated that most popular singers had better find a secure place by the age of fifty, since by seventy-five they are grazing in the pastures of retirement. Frank has certainly defied that truism. The *Times* wrote of his sheer physical presence, imperial glare, and ominous, gripping volatility, and praised his "chilling power and authority."

He performed in a boxing ring from which the ropes had been removed. Seated in the front row, I was close by when he started his ascent into the ring. As he reached the top step a roar rang out from twenty thousand throats. He stood silently for a moment, as a tribute to his place in the history of popular singers pounded down on him. Those present were representing millions of Americans for whom a Sinatra song has been meaningful at one time or another in their lives. His performance thrilled the crowd from first to last. It was a moving tribute to the long road he has traveled. The evening will always be the highlight of our fifty years of friendship.

A week earlier in Los Angeles the Society of Singers had paid him a unique, emotional salute as a parade of singers, most of them popular earlier in his career, each sang one song in tribute to him.

One evening during that week we had dinner together. We reminisced about our decade at the Sinatra compound. Our eyes grew a little misty. My, what wonderful times we had.

# ME
## *and*
# ROBERT TAYLOR

IN 1943 the United States Navy had approximately eighty thousand officers. I was one. Robert Taylor, certifiable world-class MGM film star, was another. The chance of his playing an important role in my life was too minuscule to calculate. Even the sophisticated computers that would come on stream decades later would spit it out.

We beat the odds. I was assigned to Navy Public Relations and specifically to "The Navy Hour," a radio program devoted to dramatizing naval heroes. There was a constant search for big names to host the show, and they came up with a winner in Lieutenant Junior Grade Robert Taylor, who was stationed at a stateside naval base. The program originated in Washington. It was my job to shepherd him through the process, which is where I first met him. He was quiet, pleasant, and reserved, all qualities that went unnoticed because he was so breathtakingly handsome.

He did his stint and we flew to New York in a Navy plane. He was scheduled to do a second program in a week and seemed unreasonably despondent about spending the intervening time in a New York hotel. I said, innocently enough, "There must be worse things than being Robert Taylor and having a free week in New York City." "Not for me," he said firmly. "I can't leave my room without being mobbed. I'm a prisoner, plain and simple. I don't have any friends in New York and my only telephone calls will be to room service." I told him I had a Park Avenue apartment and suggested that he stay with me, where no room service calls would be required. He said quietly that he did not want to impose, but I gave him my telephone number just in case and we made plans to meet the following week for another trek to Washington.

Three days later he called and said he would like to take me up on my offer if it was still open. I assured him it was and quickly acquired a lonesome movie star boarder. He could not have been easier or more appreciative. He was disappointed that his wife, Barbara Stanwyck, could not join him for that week, but she was filming. To my disappointment, he was totally uncommunicative about his glamorous Hollywood life. When we did try to go beyond the confines of the apartment I realized his dilemma. He had already made, among other outstanding films, *Magnificent Obsession* with Irene Dunne and been dubbed by *Time* as "the most admired matinee idol since the late Rudolph Valentino." Anywhere he went he was instantly surrounded and, although he knew it went with the territory, he disliked it.

Cary Grant, in describing himself, said it best. "There was no such thing as a Cary Grant until I invented him." There certainly was no such thing as a Robert Taylor until he was invented. Spangler Arlington Brugh, not Robert Taylor, was born in 1911 in Nebraska. His roots were deep and his values were set long before his good looks came to the attention of talent scouts and he made the transition to Robert Taylor, California resident and film star. The transplantation never really took with Bob. He found his life seductive and remunerative, but he could never quite get rid of the feeling that wearing costumes and makeup was not a proper way for a man to earn a living. It was too bad since he simply was incapable of getting enjoyment from achieving a very high pinnacle of success and being the idol of untold millions of people.

Bob did one more "Navy Hour" program and then returned to his base. He had been the pleasantest of houseguests, and my stock with the elevator operators, doormen, and other tenants of the building shot sky-high.

Amazingly, soon after the war ended and I was back at my Wall Street job I received a call from none other than Bob Taylor in California. He and his wife were coming to New York. How did I feel about theatre and dinner afterward? I said I'd love it. He sent me my ticket and we met at the theatre. Luckily I went early. The arrival of my hosts produced massive

aisle-jamming that was contained only by the rise of the curtain.

Getting away from that theatre was far more hazardous than
any experience I had in the Navy. With the help of a policeman
and the doorman, we were stuffed into their limo. Before police
reinforcements arrived in sufficient number to let the driver
inch his way out of this unholy mess, the densely packed crowd
rocked the car and hammered the windows to the point where
I truly feared for our safety. It would have been a glamorous
way to go, but I preferred a postponement.

We had supper in the Cub Room at the city's posh Stork
Club. The patrons were used to celebrities and, for the most
part, did not approach the table. But the ogling at these two
people was truly Major League. The Stork Club was a favorite
hangout of mine. I was always well treated, but after that
evening I received the same obsequious attention that I now
commanded at my apartment.

Stanwyck, she of the sexy voice and sultry looks, was far
more outgoing than Bob. Her only interest in the evening,
after all, was helping her husband reciprocate for hospitality.
I loved her salty style and gave her an A-plus for effort. We
parted with the time-honored "Let's do this again" dialogue.

I was an instant, if momentary, celebrity. None of this,
however, made me yearn for the glamorous life covered by
the magical word "Hollywood," which seemed as foreign to
me as Tibet. Besides, I had a mighty fine lifestyle of my own.
Age thirty-three, I was gainfully employed by a top-line Wall
Street firm, a job that I got through pull. I worked at it dutifully
but without focus. The pleasures New York nightlife offered
a not impoverished young man were so seductive and diverse
that it was often a challenge for me to answer the opening bell.
Many times I would dash home to my splendid bachelor pad,
shower, change, and rush to make it on time, although office
hours were the dullest part of my existence, but it was not a
situation that cried out for change.

Destiny did not remain out of the picture. As part of my
nightly rounds I attended a great many dinner parties. One
evening I met a man named Dore Schary, a genuine Hollywood
big-shot executive. Less than ten years my senior, he had al-

ready written and produced many films and was at that moment in time head of production at RKO Studios. During the course of the evening he told me casually that if I wanted to come to California he would give me an apprenticeship, and if all went well let me try my hand at producing. He said it lightly and I took it lightly. I met him several times subsequently and invariably he repeated his offer. He was a serious man and I realized that this was not an opportunity that he tossed around on a daily basis and should be considered as a unique opportunity. Eventually I wrote him about it and again received a very positive response. With considerable and understandable trepidation I finally decided to give it a try. I traveled to California in the accepted deluxe manner, taking the 20th Century Limited to Chicago and the famous Super Chief to Los Angeles, and very comfortable it was. Within two days I was an employee at RKO and had started my training program.

Why Dore Schary chose to give me this opportunity will always remain a mystery to me. He and his family virtually adopted me, and as long as his own star remained in the ascendancy he was a father figure who was kind and instructive. My only regret is that this all fell into my lap so easily that I never quite appreciated the uniqueness of it.

The plan was to spend time in each of the departments that comprise a motion picture studio. By sheer chance I began in the location department. The logistics of this location were very simple. RKO was filming a romantic comedy, *Mr. Blandings Builds His Dream House,* starring Cary Grant, and the dream house was in Malibu. I reported at the RKO gate at five-thirty in the morning and rode to Malibu with the crew. That routine lasted only two or three days when Grant noticed me observing the proceedings. I had gotten to know him through mutual friends on his frequent trips to New York. Very surprised, he asked me how I happened to be there. When I told him he said, "Why, my boy, this is marvelous. I have an excellent idea. Why don't I have my car pick you up in the morning before they come for me and we'll ride out together. That seems much simpler." I expressed grave doubts as to how this would sit with my newly found colleagues, but Cary pooh-

poohed all of it. "Besides," he told me, "you'll learn much more riding with me than on that bus." I felt a little discomfort at first but adjusted easily. Cary was, even at that early hour, charming and solicitous. And he was right; he did teach me more than I could have learned on the bus. Once while he was studying his script he looked up and said, "Spend most of your time reading these things. Everything comes from that." I would get out of the limo a few yards before our arrival and skulk in to mingle with the others. Nothing bad came of it. My benefactor was, of course, the quintessential man of the movies. I am reasonably blasé about film stars, but although I saw him quite regularly over the years I always felt like a tourist.

I was about to move to another department when everything came to a screeching halt. Howard Hughes bought RKO Studios. One of his first acts was to fire Schary, who was immediately hired as head of production by Metro-Goldwyn-Mayer, the industry giant. I told Schary that, to put it mildly, he owed me nothing and urged him to start at MGM with no excess baggage. He was adamant and, in fact, expanded my function. I would be his assistant, serving as a buffer and general factotum. The goal of becoming a producer would remain unchanged. The result was that only a few months after arriving in California I was, in true Hollywood fashion, assistant to the MGM production head. I occupied a small, pleasant office immediately adjoining Schary's large, pleasant office.

The glory days of the major studios were beginning to wind down, but it was still a spectacular experience for an uninitiated newcomer. Clark Gable, Ava Gardner, Fred Astaire, Elizabeth Taylor, Spencer Tracy, Gene Kelly, Katharine Hepburn, and many others roamed the streets and the sound stages, bearing daily testimony to the MGM slogan that they possessed "more stars than there are in the heavens," and of course there was my former houseguest, Robert Taylor. I had not looked him up, since all too often in my own life I have had people to whom I had been polite and civil get in touch with me to say they were in town. It's a shorthand method of saying, "I'm here. Please entertain me."

My days were varied and busy. I spent time observing the

activities of the various departments, cutting, production, set design, wardrobe, and all the other units that enabled this busy film factory to send some forty films annually into the world market. I was given endless screenplays to read and each evening I saw the daily rushes with Schary.

My work as his assistant was time-consuming and could not be categorized as hardship duty. One morning, for example, his secretary ushered Bob Taylor into my office, murmuring apologetically that Mr. Schary was running a few minutes late. Taylor was, quite naturally, shocked and when I told him how I had gotten from the Stork Club to this office so quickly he was flabbergasted. We had only a few minutes to talk before Clark Gable, who had been in Schary's office, joined us. Gable had several screenplays in his hand and Bob said, "I see the new boy gave you some stuff to read." Gable grunted a laconic affirmative and Bob said, "Well, if you don't like it I'll be reading it soon." Gable went out to the reception room and Bob went into Schary's office.

Bob and Barbara, I must say, went a great deal further than they had any obligation to do on my behalf. It was largely through their efforts that I changed from being an outsider to being an insider among a group of people where status meant much and I possessed little.

After a few months Schary called me into his office and told me that he had a project for me to produce. It was a Western called *Ambush,* due to be published six months later in the *Saturday Evening Post,* a magazine that was then a huge source of material to the studios. He wished me luck in a fatherly, confident manner and I was shortly moved into a large suite with my own bathroom and, infinitely more important, my own secretary, who is with me to this day. Producers rated high on the MGM totem pole and the roads to producership were numerous. They came from the ranks of writers and cutters, from the stage, from talent agencies and unceasingly from the happy, unbridled custom of nepotism. Sitting in my leather chair that first morning I thought, and still think, that my route was quite unique and magical.

I had been told that my salary would be one thousand dollars; I thought this meant a month and I was thrilled. This elation was compounded when my first check arrived. I was being paid one thousand dollars per week. In those days, when a dollar was a dollar, it seemed not too shabby for someone who still considered not getting lost on the giant lot something of a victory. I immediately went to the office of my good friend Sam Zimbalist, one of the top producers, and told him about it. His reaction was immediate. "Are those cheapskates only paying you a thousand dollars a week?" he asked. "You've got to insist on a raise." I told him that a raise was the last thing that I wanted or expected and that I would have been perfectly content with much less. I also reminded him that as a producer I was now entitled to daily free lunch of the highest quality in the executive dining room. He expressed grave doubts about my ability to survive in this jungle and said that such a measly salary struck a blow to all producers. I left his office unconvinced and ecstatic.

I did not often avail myself of the executive dining room. The prestige was high and the food excellent. However, it was no match for the commissary, which was without doubt the most colorful place on the entire lot. It was for the sole use of MGM employees and it definitely had a clubby feeling. Handsome men and beautiful women lunching there in every imaginable kind of costume and in full makeup gave it the festive air of a fancy dress party. These were, of course, all the Metro stars filming at the time.

One day early on Bob Taylor came in and sat down opposite me. He was in costume and makeup and made me feel as though I had just come out from under a manhole. I said to him, "Goddamn it, it just doesn't seem right that I work so hard and you look so great." His answer, made casually, was prophetic, "You can look like you look forever," he said, "and I can only look like this for a few years."

*Ambush* seemed just fine to me. It was certainly not the kind of project assigned to the front-rank producers, but had the makings of a respectable program film to be produced with second-tier stars and a competent director. I quickly received a call from the Story Department that Marguerite Roberts had been assigned to write the screenplay. She was an excellent MGM contract writer with over twenty fine credits who normally drew more important assignments. Fortunately for me, she happened to be available and shortly appeared in my sumptuous quarters for the first of a series of story conferences that would incorporate my views before she started the actual writing.

This was normal procedure, but this was obviously a special situation involving a veteran writer and a neophyte producer. On the spur of the moment I told Maggie that my contribution to these story conferences would necessarily be minimal and perhaps counterproductive. I suggested that she get on with the writing of the screenplay and asked her to take an oath in blood that she would keep this unconventional type of collaboration to herself. Most writers regard story conferences as a waste of time and she gave me her promise instantly. Unlike Sam Zimbalist, she told me fervently that she thought I had the makings of an excellent producer.

The screenplay was completed very quickly because we had skipped the story conference period and Maggie knew what she wanted from the beginning. It seemed first-rate to me. We did not want to give the impression that it had been dashed off, so we held it back for a few weeks and then sent it along to Schary. A series of conferences with him was the next order of business. He liked it very much but naturally had a lot of suggestions, none of which appealed to Maggie. She urged me as the producer to fight for "our" story points. This did not appeal to me at all. My checks were coming regularly. My office was now filled with pictures and photographs. My backhand had improved markedly during the writing of the script and I wanted no flak.

I countered by suggesting that, because of Schary's work load, we would be wise to make all the changes he requested and gradually restore the original material without anyone being the wiser. She agreed and so it was that the often torturous effort of getting ready to move forward with a finished screenplay was accomplished with no trauma and very speedily indeed. I received compliments on this maiden effort, which I accepted modestly, leaving the definite impression, however, that my contribution had not been unimportant.

And so it was that *Ambush* was sent to mimeograph, and

very quickly I became the proud possessor of six yellow-covered copies, each proclaiming me as the producer. A rather low-key period followed this exhilarating moment. The script was sent to the Production Department, whose job it was to break down the cost of making the movie on a scene-by-scene basis. Crises and top priorities governed their lives, so I was resigned to the fact that my program picture would go through the mill like glue.

My glue had no chance to harden. My secretary buzzed me to announce that Bob Taylor was in the reception room. We were friends by now, but still it seemed odd. In MGM's stratified hierarchy major stars had no need to cruise around the offices of fledgling producers. He came in, sat down, lit a cigarette, and told me that he had a problem.

It had already been announced that Bob was slated to head an all-star cast in Dore Schary's personal production of *Battleground*. He felt his career at that point in time needed a personal starring vehicle. He asked me if I, as a close friend of Schary's, would plead his case. I immediately responded that I could see nothing for me to gain by telling Schary that his leading man wanted out and suggested that he let his agent carry these hot coals.

During the course of all this his eye fell upon the small stack of yellow-covered scripts on my otherwise empty desk. He asked about it and I told him with unabashed pride that these were the first copies of my initial effort as a producer. Bob said he would like to read it. I told him forcefully it was out of the question. MGM's method of script distribution to its top personalities was as rigid and unswerving as a minuet. Every detail was carefully orchestrated, and the star's agent was the conduit. It was totally outside the system for a neophyte producer to personally give a screenplay to the likes of Robert Taylor. I could not have been more emphatic. He responded by casually picking a copy of the screenplay off my desk. "Bullshit," he said. "Don't make such a big deal out of it. We're friends. I'll just read it and get it back to you in the morning."

True to his word, he called me the next morning and informed me that he loved the script and planned to get out of

*Battleground* to star in it. My reaction was immediate. I told him that I had no intention of setting out on a course which would terminate my job instantly and that I would come to his house forthwith and pick up the script. I did just that, reminding him again in very forceful terms not to tinker with my newfound, pleasant life. He agreed, but did tell me that it had been a long time since a producer had been so vociferous about not wanting him in a film.

Driving back to the studio, visions of sugar plums danced in my head. For several days and nights I tried to envisage some method of snaking Robert Taylor out of my boss's picture and into mine. It seemed to me to be in the true spirit of Hollywood, but I was not creative enough to come up with a risk-free way of doing it. Each elaborate scheme wound up with me in front of Schary's desk and hearing him say, "You're fired, you ungrateful son of a bitch."

I tried to think no more about it, but it was as futile as having Elizabeth Taylor ask you to take her away for the weekend and replying that, for certain reasons, it would not be practicable. One might not go on the weekend, but it was not possible to put it out of one's mind.

Several weeks passed uneventfully before I was next summoned to Schary's office. I had received the preliminary budget and presumed that this would be the subject of the meeting, together with some casting ideas. When I arrived I was stunned to see that the only other person present was Bob Taylor's agent. I sank into the first available chair. Schary, the man who had given me such generous and unlimited opportunity, informed me briefly that Bob had read *Ambush* and was eager to do it. He said that the studio had decided after considerable thought to accede to his request. Bob's agent got up to leave. As he walked out he turned to me and said briefly, "You're a lucky guy," to which I agreed weakly but fervently. I tried to follow him out but Schary stopped me at the door. The matter of how Taylor happened to acquire the screenplay hung heavily in the air between us. What seemed like an eternity passed before Schary impassively echoed the agent's comments, "You're a lucky guy." Again I agreed.

I headed back to my office, my mind dwelling on the evident

virtues of duplicity. Although I had been told to say nothing about it until the studio announced it, I could not resist calling Maggie Roberts in confidence with the news. Her surprise was total and she said to me, quite naturally, "How did it come about?" I replied that it was, after all, an excellent screenplay. I made some vague comments about kismet and left her with the feeling that a firm hand was at the tiller.

The front-office choice of director was uppermost in my mind and I was not kept waiting long to get the news. I was summoned to Schary's office. He told me that Sam Wood liked the story, liked the script, liked Robert Taylor and would direct the film. Wood's reputation was legendary. He had directed over fifty films, including such famous hits as *Goodbye, Mr. Chips, Our Town, Kitty Foyle, Kings Row, Pride of the Yankees, For Whom the Bell Tolls,* and *Saratoga Trunk.*

Schary told me that I must prepare myself for the possibility that I would be removed from the project since there were many front-rank producers with whom Wood had worked previously and none of whom would be wasted on a Robert Taylor film. Stricken, I asked Schary if he would allow a thing like this to happen and he said quietly that he might very well accede to Sam Wood's wishes. The similarity of his choice of words to the Bob Taylor episode did not escape me and I slunk out, having gone from the top to the bottom in less than thirty seconds.

I decided that I had little to lose and I would take my best shot at Mr. Wood, whom I did not know but who had a reputation of being crusty, direct, and cantankerous. I phoned him and asked for an appointment. It was agreed we would meet in his office the next morning. I also correctly identified Taylor as the source of my problem. I called him and told him bitterly that he had managed to transform the nice little picture that I was going to produce into a nice big picture which I was not going to produce. I appeared very promptly indeed, after a totally sleepless night. The directors' building was a ramshackle affair compared to the producers' building and Sam Wood's office was microscopic compared to my own. When I entered, I found Bob Taylor was sitting quietly on the sofa. I introduced myself to Mr. Wood and with hardly a moment's preamble plunged headlong into the whole saga of events that had taken me from the dinner party in New York all the way to his office in an incredibly short period of time.

Without shame I pleaded for this opportunity, telling him that it might not come to me again for years. I assured him that he need expect no trouble from me. I would shine his shoes, get his lunch, back him to the hilt in everything, and even try to get Bob to play the girl if that's what he wanted. The end of this twenty-minute peroration inevitably arrived and I only had to wait a second before he said, "You'll do. Most producers are stupid as hell anyway. You couldn't be any worse than they are." I offered my hand gratefully and he took it reluctantly. I thanked him and left, stealing a side glance at Taylor, who sat impassively, the inevitable cigarette in his hand. Taylor would never admit it, but there is no doubt in my mind that he had saved my bacon.

The Location Department decided that the area around Gallup, New Mexico, was the most promising place to scout for our locations and dispatched a team of still photographers. Some ten days later I looked at their results with Sam. To me it was an almost euphoric moment. I no longer had to read the script direction, "The Indians come riding through the pass." I could actually see the pass where this would happen. Nothing was on the screen yet, but it was getting there. Sam, however, had a more jaundiced eye. After careful study he proclaimed, "Those bastards must have been reading a different script. I'll have to go out and get these myself."

He returned with a batch of stills that, to my untrained eye, looked amazingly like the first ones, although I assured him that the differences were profound. "Just once," he said vindictively, "these guys should be forced to actually try and shoot film from their stills. The studio would save a fortune."

Pre-production activity picked up speed daily. This part of filmmaking can, on occasion, be so attenuated that it becomes tedious. However, due to the studio's desire to get a Robert Taylor–Sam Wood film finished and released all signs were "Go" for us and certain other projects were temporarily put on a siding as our express sped through.

I was with Sam from early morning to late evening. Actors

were interviewed, sketches for sets and wardrobe approved, locations selected, budgets and shooting schedules settled after intense arguments.

Sam's attitude toward me in front of others never varied. The charade that we were equal partners in the decision-making process was meticulously observed by him. "I guess this is okay," he would say of a costume sketch, and then to me, "What do you think?" or, after seeing a dozen actors for a small part he'd tell our casting director, "I don't think any of them are quite right but we'll talk about it and let you know." His courtesy was unswerving and unobtrusive. Taylor noticed this while checking out his own wardrobe. He grinned surreptitiously and winked at me. During these hectic weeks I grew very fond of Sam. I had no way of expressing my gratitude. Any word of this sort would have brought from him a swift and snarling denial.

We had only one brief flare-up. Arlene Dahl was assigned to the picture. Sam wanted a much bigger box-office name than Arlene and, like Marguerite Roberts, told me it was my duty to mount a full-scale attack on the front office. "Those bastards," he said, "will walk all over you if you let them. There are plenty of stars on this lot who aren't doing a damn thing right now but drawing their pay. It's up to you to take a firm stand." Feeling extremely insecure about making firm stands, I telephoned Bob Taylor immediately for advice, which came quickly. "Don't fight with the front office about this. You'll lose. The part isn't strong enough for a big star and Sam knows it. He's just been too nice to you and wants you to suffer a little. He's the one to stand up to, not the front office." Wood growled and grumbled about my unwillingness to mount an attack, but in the end he was surprisingly docile, realizing that the part did not merit Greta Garbo. "You're getting to be a real producer very quickly," he commented, "unwilling and unable to do a goddamn thing."

Six weeks later Sam and I left for Gallup, followed shortly by the entire cast and crew plus many freight cars loaded down with props and equipment. The sight of these freight cars compared with my ride west on the Super Chief neatly framed my feeling of unreality about all that had happened to me in less than two years since I decided on a whim to go to California.

Filming on location can be a miserable process replete with delays, recriminations, violent unpleasantness, temperament, and worse. My lucky star continued in the ascendancy. Bob Taylor and Sam Wood were both consummate professionals. Bob arrived on time, knew his lines, and was skilled in his role. Wood had his day's work planned. His gruff monosyllabic instructions to cast and crew inspired confidence. No one thought *Ambush* would be another *Gone With the Wind,* but everyone felt it was destined to be a success.

Understatement was Wood's forte. The climactic ambush sequence called for several dozen Indians to bury themselves in gravelike holes in the ground. The ambush occurred as the Army rode in and the Indians sprang up, killing the entire detachment except, fortunately, the scout Robert Taylor, who had resolutely opposed the tactic. As the Indians buried themselves for the scene, Sam turned to his assistant and said, "Make sure these air holes are big enough. This thing won't work if those guys suffocate."

*Ambush* returned to the studio on time and on budget with the complexities and daily frustrations of moviemaking still totally unknown to me. The sets which had been sketched were now on studio sound stages for the finish of shooting, and one day, perhaps thirty-eight days after the troupe left for Gallup, the production was completed. We had a pro forma party on the set and then all the people who had grown so close to one another scattered and waited for the next film.

The night that we went out for our first preview at a local theatre I was, in the true tradition, a nervous wreck. I had not forgotten the strange juxtaposition of events that brought me to that evening; but somehow, for a few hours I was able to forget the contribution of others. When I saw my name on the screen my pleasure was so pure and overwhelming that I had little left to judge the strength and weaknesses of the film. It didn't matter. Few first previews go as well as that one did and the subsequent changes were minor indeed.

In 1950 *Ambush* was released, aided and abetted by a generous advertising and publicity campaign. It was just what all the people on location felt it would be, entertaining and successful. In short, a marvelous first credit for a new producer who happened to attend a dinner party less than two years before in New York.

I did not wait too long before going again to Sam Zimbalist's office. I told him that now I was going to ask for a raise. He urged me not to do it, saying that I should have done it when he suggested it and that it would be better to wait at least a year. We wound up making a rather sizable bet and off I went to the office of Eddie Mannix, the executive who held sway over these matters. Mannix was a warm, mercurial Irishman, famous for his tough exterior. When I told him why I was there he got red in the face and asked me by what right I had the nerve to ask after making only one film.

I decided that my policy of telling the truth had stood me in good stead and told him of my bet with Zimbalist. He allowed that the picture was doing pretty well and said he'd give me a $250-a-week raise and I was to get the hell out of there and not show up for a long time. I remember now walking toward Zimbalist's office to collect my bet. What, I wondered, was hard about the picture business?

My first picture was, regrettably, Sam Wood's last. He died a few months later, leaving behind him a marvelous body of film work. I was saddened by his passing, though the closeness which we developed during that comparatively brief period ended with the conclusion of the film. Not so with Bob Taylor. We were friends before the picture and remained friends afterward.

In 1952 Bob Taylor and Barbara Stanwyck were divorced after thirteen years of marriage. Certainly divorce was prevalent throughout America, but these superstar marriages had so much to combat that they seemed doomed from the start. There is a constant drumbeat of publicity pouring out from the studios and the press agents to the media, all so positive and upbeat that it takes on a life of its own. Smiling photographs at previews, laughing photographs at parties with other beautiful, smiling people, and interviews with the principals about the unblemished blessedness of married life. It seemed as though the gods felt compelled to fight the press agents and inform people that their presentation of these lives is a hoax. The truth of the matter was that Taylor and Stanwyck had all the same strains on their relationship that other people had, in addition to long, forced separations for filming which often strained the marriage vows beyond the limit. Underlying this particular breakup was a difference in outlook. Stanwyck had no trouble at all in transforming herself from Ruby Stevens of the New York chorus to Barbara Stanwyck of Beverly Hills, the movies, and particularly the social life, which did not appeal to Bob. She pressed for a divorce, got it, and for the rest of her life regarded it as her greatest mistake.

In 1958 we made another western, *Saddle the Wind,* together. Four years earlier Bob had met and married Ursula Thiess, a German-born beauty, a union that set in motion what would be the happiest period of his life. This location was in Colorado and we naturally resumed the custom of our nightly dinners together. It was not difficult to observe that professionally Bob felt, and with reason, on shaky ground. He had made almost sixty films by then and could not shake a strong sense of melancholy and *déjà vu.*

Gary Cooper, a pragmatic sage on the subject, once commented that one good picture out of five was enough to keep the old bicycle wheel turning. When we made *Ambush,* Bob's bicycle was pumping away at a much brisker clip than that. Since then he had certainly made some marvelous movies, including *Ivanhoe* and *Quo Vadis,* but the ratio of outstanding work was slowly declining below the Cooper formula. *Saddle the Wind,* strictly a program picture, was no help. I tried to buoy him up a bit one evening and his reply was succinct and to the point. "Book a projection room at the studio," he said, "and run *Camille.*" He made a few more films after that, but the inevitable downward curve continued. His passing comment to me a decade ago in the commissary about his looks was prophetic. Although he was still a fine-looking man, the chiseled features that the camera had loved so well were blurred.

About that time Bob and Ursula bought a ranch-style house and acreage in Mandeville Canyon, still countrified today but then a truly rural area. Here an idyllic period set in. Metro-

Goldwyn-Mayer, home base for his enormous climb to stardom, was only twenty minutes away. The social scene in which he had been such an active part was just as close, but it was almost as if the two of them had returned to Nebraska. They saw very few of Bob's old friends. They lived quietly and rode a lot of horseback. They had two children and raised them to know as little as possible of their father's legendary years.

Hundreds of thousands of transplanted Midwesterners migrated to Southern California in that era, never really surrendering the basic values they had brought with them. Bob became one of them, not separated from them by Hollywood and superstardom. He had never sought dizzying heights or aspired to being made into Robert Taylor. With Ursula he happily found again his very real, very unshakable roots.

Bob died in 1969 of lung cancer. I do not recall ever seeing him without a cigarette, but it was to be some years before any of his friends recognized the correlation between the two. His funeral service inevitably took on all the trappings of superstardom. There were fans and policemen and a long cortege. Ronald Reagan, newly elected to his first term as Governor of California and a close friend of Bob's, spoke the eulogy. I was proud to be selected as a pallbearer.

I treasure to this day a picture taken on the set of *Ambush* at an impromptu birthday party for Bob. The studio brass attended and Bob was flanked by Sam Wood on one side and me on the other. Sam looked, and was, annoyed at the interruption of the shooting schedule. Taylor tried to look surprised and pleased as he cut the cake. My own expression mirrored the quizzical disbelief I had felt from the beginning.

Hollywood! What fantasy, what glamour that name evokes. Untold millions try desperately to climb the wall and get on the inside of this magical world. Bob and I certainly shared one thing in common. The wall, like the Berlin Wall, came down for us and we walked in with no effort at all.

# ME

*and*

# MY FAVORITE ACTOR

LOUIS CALHERN, my favorite actor, loved his profession and was inordinately proud to be part of it. From the late 1920s to the mid-1950s he roamed the stages and screens of America. He appeared in over forty plays, most of them as a full-fledged star, and some seventy films where, with one exception, he was a strong supporting player. He was tall, handsome, debonair, wore clothes as though to the manner born, and supported a beautifully groomed Guardsman's moustache. He was a superb raconteur. The warmth and quality of his friendship was high indeed.

All of these attributes applied to him in spades when he was sober. When he was drunk it was an entirely different matter. He fought alcohol all his life, winning some and losing some. Coping with his defeats could be a real trial, since the smell of the cork of a bottle of Dubonnet could set him off. Conversely, he enjoyed long periods of sobriety. I met him early on and quickly realized that if one was to be his friend those conditions were the only ground rules available. I accepted them and, though sorely tested, never regretted it.

His life was filled with adventures and misadventures. For example, in 1932 he wandered into a New York saloon. He was, as he liked to put it, "off the wagon," so on the surface that was not an unusual move. This watering hole, however, was unique, advertising itself as the city's longest bar. It cut through an entire block. There was only one customer leaning against it. Calhern pressed close to this man and said loudly, "Move over, you big fag." The man he was leaning on was Tom Heeney, current heavyweight champion of the world, who promptly shoved Calhern through a plywood wall, leaving him decked but unharmed. The two men spent what was left of the night together. It was the unlikely beginning of a friendship. Heeney always invited Calhern to see him fight in the old Madison Square Garden.

Calhern was a knowledgeable sports fan, so it always annoyed me that when boxing was brought up he pronounced Heeney as one of America's greatest heavyweight champions. In truth, he was to the heavyweight championship what Millard Fillmore was to the U.S. Presidency. He could not have gone three rounds with the likes of Joe Louis or Muhammad Ali. Calhern remained immovable on the subject. He had a great gift for friendship.

New York and the theatre were his true loves, but in 1950 his performance in John Huston's superb film *The Asphalt Jungle* was so outstanding that Metro-Goldwyn-Mayer offered him a contract he could not refuse. He had not always been complimentary about Hollywood, but Broadway was getting increasingly chancy and the timing and the money were right. I had known him in New York, but our close friendship flourished when he pulled up stakes to live in the California sunshine, which he hated.

We soon made a habit to lunch together in the commissary. In the evening we frequently dropped in to the welcoming open house maintained for over twenty-five years by the superb lyricist, the late Ira Gershwin and his wife, Lee. It was a warm, gracious salon for the creative community, and particularly appreciated by newly arrived homesick outlanders from New York like Calhern. I cherish to this day the fact that I was welcome at the Gershwins'. Our last stop was at Calhern's house and it was there that he held forth with relish and gusto.

His lips were tightly sealed about his many conquests, but he did, "out of the kindness of his heart," advise me how to conduct my newly acquired bachelor life. "The key," he emphasized, "is that all sexual encounters must take place away from your own home. Otherwise the lady is apt to stay on far too long and there is no polite way to get rid of her."

By way of illustration he gave me in lugubrious detail an example of the inevitable pitfalls if this golden rule was broken. One night he took to his New York hotel a lady he could not wait to possess. Later he felt an equally strong urge to be alone.

Feeling cozy and comfortable, she showed no signs of leaving. Calhern finally felt he had no alternative but to get dressed himself. The lady, lying languorously in his bed, asked, not without reason, what he was up to. He said, "I must get out of here. I feel I am falling in love with you." He left his apartment and the night clerk gave him another room. He did not return to his own diggings until he was positive that his latest conquest had departed.

By the time he settled in California Calhern had gone through quite a number of briskly paced marriages and divorces. His wives had much in common with one another. They were high-profile, brittle, chic, witty, and attractive. All of them obviously met him during a sober period and, totally charmed by him, convinced themselves they could change him. After living through a few of his bouts with the bottle they understandably grew disillusioned. Natalie Schaefer, a fine actress, sent to her successor, the actress and writer Ilka Chase, some "Mr. and Mrs. Louis Calhern" informals with a brief note: "Ilka dear: Use these quickly." Calhern bore these ladies no rancor and they remained friends with one another and with him.

His Ethel Barrymore stories were a treasure trove. These two worthies often toured the hinterland together in distinguished plays enjoying excellent box-office results. Miss Barrymore was properly hailed as the Great Lady of the theatre, but in the family tradition, she was a first-class toper whose pattern of sobriety and drinking paralleled Calhern's. Early on they devised a system that worked beautifully if one member of the duo remained sober. The sober one would say his own lines, following with the phrase, "And if I were you I know what I would say," and then recite the other person's lines. Although it became a soliloquy, their fame and regal stage presence made it work.

When they were both drunk at the same performance it was traumatic. Calhern recalled a night they were both standing numb and silent on a stage. The only voice to be heard was that of the prompter loudly offering up the next line. Finally an annoyed Miss Barrymore turned toward the prompter and said clearly, "We know the line, young man. Who says it?"

For Calhern the upside was the money. The downside was the touring stage managers, necessary evils whose twin missions in life were to keep him sober and on time as the tours wended their way through medium-sized, boring cities. He was therefore not surprised to be awakened one morning and queried as to how he had ever been able to get through last night's performance. Before he had a chance to pull himself together, the stage manager continued, "Miss Barrymore was so drunk I just don't know how you made it." Enormously relieved, Calhern immediately became his magnanimous, helpful self. "It happens," he said. "We must all do our best to help her. You can count on me." Twenty seconds later he was sleeping the deep sleep of the innocent.

Like many others before me, I occasionally felt that Calhern had successfully conquered his demons, which was rather like believing in the tooth fairy. I was awakened late one night by a telephone call from Howard Keel, MGM actor, singer, and golfer par excellence. Keel had dropped by Calhern's home, as was the custom of a few good friends, to find him "off the wagon" with a vengeance. I arrived there with all possible speed. Our debonair friend was staggering about, highly abusive and threatening to go out on the town. I told Keel that the time had come to end the evening. Howard regretfully delivered a very gentle, precise knockout tap to the chin. Thanks to Dr. Keel's nonbarbiturate potion, Calhern was sleeping soundly before we got him into bed.

He was shooting a film, so I appeared on the set bright and early the next morning to inform the director that Calhern was under the weather. My meaning was absolutely clear. I was assured that all concerned would do their best to cover for him. Their best, however, was not good enough. MGM kept close tabs on absent actors, always aware of the old maxim that the studios conducted the only business in the world where the inventory went home every night. By noon the studio doctor, appropriately named Dr. Blank, was at Calhern's home and reported to the appropriate authorities that the actor was "sleeping it off." Calhern got off with a very light reprimand, due largely to the fact that I had covered all bases with dexterity.

Any thought that he would be grateful proved totally incorrect. He appeared unannounced in my office a day later, debonair, confident, Guardsman moustache *au point*. Without preamble he said angrily, "You're the son of a bitch who snitched to the studio, aren't you?" Controlling my urge to hit him far harder than Keel had, I said that I had acted as an agent without fee. That ended it. We chatted briefly, then made a dinner date before he jauntily departed. A cloud no bigger than a man's fist had appeared in the blue sky. I failed to observe it and would live to regret it later.

For several years I had been pleading with the front office to acquire the film rights to *The Magnificent Yankee,* which had been a highly successful play based on the life of the distinguished Supreme Court Justice Oliver Wendell Holmes. It starred none other than Louis Calhern, whose performance had been widely acclaimed, yielding him numerous awards. I had, in fact, been Calhern's guest at the opening night and had an abiding faith in the material.

The top studio executives had justifiable doubts about the subject matter. They also felt that with the title, *The Magnificent Yankee,* audiences would expect to see the life of Babe Ruth. To a man they doubted Calhern's ability to carry a motion picture. I kept pestering everyone from Louis B. Mayer on down, pounding at the fact that the rights could be acquired cheaply and the picture made on a small budget. Finally, having had enough of me, they caved in. Not thinking I would prevail, I had never mentioned the matter to Calhern. The idea of getting his hopes up and then dashing them made me shiver.

Once it was a done deal I told him. He was at first unbelieving, then overwhelmed. It was more than he had ever dared hope. I have never before or since been the subject of such lavish praise. The legendary Irving Thalberg was, he said, a B-picture maker compared to me. A man of my showmanship was certain to be ranked with the all-time great producers.

The truth was that he had been playing more than his share of Guardsmen and grand dukes, roles that he claimed favored his moustache. For a fine actor who proclaimed that he could play anything from a collie dog to a dowager empress, it was a bit galling. The mere thought of getting his teeth into a wonderful role was enough to get his adrenaline flowing. He pledged me his undying friendship and his total sobriety. I believed the first and prayed for the second.

A great many fine actresses read for the pivotal role of Mrs. Holmes. One of the unsuccessful candidates was Jessica Tandy. As I watched her legendary career unfold, it could not help but occur to me that a system which permits a superior talent of her quality to be judged by a novice producer cannot be foolproof.

The shooting of the film was a joy from start to finish. The daily rushes showed that Calhern was giving the performance of his life. Our director was first-rate. Most important, the author of the stage play adapted his work into a wonderful screenplay, capturing the Holmes story beautifully.

Holmes was a brilliant, distinguished, forceful man with a keen and sometimes biting humor. He sat on the Federal Bench with great distinction in Boston until he was sixty years old, delivering many famous opinions. He was appointed to the Supreme Court almost as a tribute to his career. It was naturally thought that he would remain a comparatively short time. He sat on the Court for thirty years and has come down as one of the most eminent Justices in history.

His life was his work, his half-century love affair with his wife, Fanny, and his relationship with his clerks. Our writer was able to get in just enough of his decisions without making them preachy. A famous example is, "A man may shout *fire* in an open field, but not in a crowded opera house. The question always is—Would the words as used create a clear and present danger to the safety of the Republic?"

The only regret that the Holmeses shared was that they were childless. Each year after he came to Washington he had a young law clerk who had distinguished himself in law school. His demands on these young men were high. When they failed to perform to his satisfaction he was harsh. Underneath one felt his affection.

To celebrate his eightieth birthday his wife secretly assembled the twenty law clerks, now distinguished lawyers or jurists on their own. The Holmeses, in evening dress to have a private celebration in their favorite restaurant, are leaving his library when he hears a murmur. The script at this point reads:

The Judge moves quickly down the room and pauses in the big doorway leading into the Secretary's room. He stops and looks off in amazement.

LONG SHOT—PAST JUDGE—INTO SECRETARY'S ROOM

Grouped in the Secretary's room in a rough semi-circle are some twenty secretaries. Some are in dinner jackets, some are in tails—all of them are men of distinction.

CLOSE SHOT—HOLMES

The Judge is deeply touched.

HOLMES

Well, I'll be blowed—the chain gang—all of 'em—

CLOSE SHOT—FANNY

She is smiling softly. She is as proud of these boys as she is of the Judge.

ANOTHER ANGLE—JUDGE AND SECRETARIES

The secretaries start to file into the library past Holmes. There is a lot of hubbub at first. "How are you, Judge" . . . "Happy birthday, sir" . . . "Many happy returns." . . .

ANOTHER ANGLE—JUDGE AND SECRETARIES

Suddenly the scene is a scene without words, except for a simple "son"—from the Judge as he greets each boy. As the last Secretary steps up to shake Holmes' hand, the word "son" can barely be heard.

In his response the Justice says, "I could not be prouder of you if you were my own sons—and you are in a way—sons at law." The look between the Justice and his wife indicates the absence of children is a thing forgotten. The scene, directed and played simply, never failed to move audiences.

The big brass, who had been so skeptical, now became overly exuberant, certain that they had a sleeper on their hands that would rack up huge grosses.

*The Magnificent Yankee* opened to rave reviews at Radio City Music Hall, then the showcase of America. It went on to do very respectable business. Everyone connected with the project modestly accepted congratulations. To cap the climax, Calhern received an Academy Award nomination. He did not win, but made no bones about the fact that it was a high point in his career.

While we were still basking in the glow of *The Magnificent Yankee,* my star burst unannounced into my office. He was in a state of high excitement, brandishing a script which he described as the finest play he had read in years. Together we would bring it to Broadway. I would be the producer, he the star and director. It was the absolute perfect vehicle to reunite us. I quickly told him that I was very happy at MGM and had not the slightest knowledge of how to produce a Broadway show. He made me promise to read it, leaving with the assurance that we were embarking on a great adventure.

*The Wooden Dish* was way before its time. It dealt with an aging man who lived with his not-too-young son and daughter-in-law, and ate from a wooden dish. Day by day he destroyed the fabric of their lives. Today he would be diagnosed as a victim of Alzheimer's disease. At that time the couple had to care for him constantly, fighting with each other in their spare time about the morality of putting him in a home.

I had great doubts about the commercial value of the play, and reminded Calhern repeatedly of his drinking problem. He had the gall at one point to tell me that if the old man was drunk it might even play better. He never let up. He fought with the same determination that I showed about *The Magnificent Yankee.* Finally I caved in and we both secured a leave of absence from MGM. Calhern felt elated since it meant that we were free to get under way. I felt as though I had been thrown out by my family.

My MGM colleagues all advised me that having Calhern as star, as well as first-time director, would make the sobriety odds very long indeed. By that time, however, I had caught Calhern's bug and we charged ahead.

Today raising the money is a daunting task. In 1953 I did not find it a challenge. The entire production was budgeted for $150,000. Units were three thousand dollars and I conservatively limited myself to one. I solicited only friends who would not be hurt by the loss of the money, assuring them that the loss was a certainty. When they asked to read the script

I refused point-blank, telling them that if they read it they would never invest. This extremely soft sell was quite effective. Several people asked if they could have two or more units, but I was adamant. We had the money within two weeks. Calhern, deft and certain, assembled a splendid cast. We opened in St. Louis to excellent notices and good business.

A lengthy tour had been scheduled before we were to open at the Booth Theatre in New York. The excellent performances revealed the need for considerable rewriting. In the theatre, unlike Hollywood, the author is king. Not a comma can be changed without his approval. Our author thought his baby was perfect. He resisted almost every suggestion, causing Calhern considerable agitation.

I kept my fingers crossed, shepherding my star around more like a keeper than a producer. It was a study in futility. I walked into the Hanna Theatre in Detroit one night to watch the proceedings from the back of the house. Calhern was off the wagon, although, as he had predicted, the old man's mumbling speech pattern masked it partially from the audience. The instant the curtain fell I sped full tilt to his dressing room. Before the door was closed I said, "You're drunk, you son of a bitch." He halfheartedly denied it. I hustled him back to the hotel. It was a silent cab ride.

We shared the elevator with two couples. One of the men timidly said that they would be honored if he would join them for a nightcap. Calhern, in his usual polite tone, replied, "I would rather bash my head against the side of this elevator wall until it was bloody than be with you for one moment." They got off at their floor feeling like lepers. I would gladly have killed Calhern with my bare hands.

He never got roaring drunk, but he never got completely sober either. We opened in New York as scheduled and closed the following Saturday. He came off adequately, but the cutting edge of his original masterful performance was gone. It naturally had a negative effect on the rest of the cast.

In retrospect I realize that it probably did not matter a bit. A brilliant performance would not have saved the day. *The Wooden Dish* was just too tough a dish to take, both for the audience and for me.

We returned to California to the welcoming arms of MGM. By common consent we avoided the subject. I grew to realize that I had made a very bad judgment call and, as usually happens, I had to pay the price. Our friendship remained intact.

I was in those days a devout Los Angeles Rams football fan and the proud possessor of two fifty-yard-line seats, so hard to come by that they were often handed down in wills.

I always took Calhern, a rabid fan and great companion. Somewhere along the way, however, he developed a strategy that I understandably found irritating. Every time the Rams made an exciting play he would say mournfully, "Do you realize that if you die before I do I'll never be able to have these seats again? It would certainly be nice if you transferred one of them into my name." I invariably told him his worries were groundless, pointing out that he was years older and that drinking was not known to promote longevity. These statements went unheeded.

Despite the fact that friends kept telling me how much he was enjoying this ploy, his constant concern for my imminent demise eventually wore me down. I finally agreed to put one seat in his name. He was elated, almost immediately appearing with the necessary paperwork, which I reluctantly signed.

We had lunch to celebrate the great ticket transfer just prior to his departure for Japan to appear in MGM's *Teahouse of the August Moon*. It would be a lengthy location, which troubled me. "Sake," I told him, "is stronger than you think. Take your cue from the title of the picture. Stick to tea." "Not to worry, my boy," he said, "my drinking days are behind me. I promise you."

This confident pledge of sobriety had an all-too-familiar ring. This time, sadly enough, he kept his word. He died suddenly in Japan before ever facing the camera. He was not off the wagon at the time, which would have pleased him mightily.

My sense of loss was great and remains so to this day. I retrieved my ticket since he had mathematically removed the possibility of my predeceasing him. The games, however, never again seemed so much fun. My interest gradually dwindled and a few years later I gave them up.

# ME

*and*

# BILLY WILDER

I HAVE MET only one man in my life who has won six motion picture Academy Awards and also sold at auction an art collection he assembled for less than one million dollars for thirty-two million dollars. Anyone who does not know Billy Wilder knows no one who meets these specifications. He is unique. *The Guinness Book of Records* should be snapping at his heels.

I am not the most objective chronicler of the ways and mores of Billy Wilder. By now our friendship stretches back almost four decades. When we first met I was a staff producer at MGM. People far above me on the motion picture ladder were in awe of him and I immediately joined an already large group. His film achievements were overwhelming and his personality, witty, urbane, and biting, dominated almost any relationship. Then too, he was older and it is not uncommon to look up to an older man.

Being with Billy under any circumstances is an excellent experience. Over the years we have lunched together on an average of once a week, and it is these luncheons stretching over time that have given me an insight into this complex man of great talent. Understanding Billy is to realize that filmmaking over the decades has been unadulterated work, contrasting totally with collecting art, which has been unadulterated pleasure.

The unvaried ritual that precedes our luncheons pleases me greatly. Almost always I make the first move by telephoning him. I am long since reconciled to this fact of life and am happy to put the ball in play. We pick the day and the restaurant. He ends the conversation by saying, "Let's double-check that morning." He is meticulous about checking and reaffirms the place. Just before we ring off he says, "Better yet, let's meet at my office."

Billy flatly refuses to ever make a reservation, which annoys me. No matter where we go he is immediately given a splendid table, which further annoys me. Once I said to him, "You must be an enormous tipper." He was genuinely surprised. "Why," he asks, "would I give the people money for simply doing their job?" He truly does not understand that he is getting special attention. A great lover of food, he is in regular communication with the captain and the maître d', who tend to hover around him, about the quality of the bread, the food, and the wine. His standard is high. If we have one mediocre meal he invariably says, "They must have changed chefs. We must remember not to come back here." Weeks later we return. If we have a fine lunch I cannot resist commenting that they must have changed chefs again, to which he replies, "Evidently." I doubt that he is aware of this entire minuet, which never fails to amuse me.

People come up to our table, call him by name, and chat with him about one thing or another. He is unfailingly courteous. When they have departed I ask him who they were. He usually says he hasn't the slightest idea, adding, "Don't you think that if I knew who they were I would have introduced them to you? Not all of us are ill-mannered." The strong inference is that I am part of a huge ill-mannered group.

His conversation is as rich and varied as are his interests. Since no man can remain a hero to his valet, my original feeling of awe should have changed. It has. It has increased. Not surprisingly, he has remained older, and by the same margin. He is now eighty-four; I am only seventy-eight.

As a young man, Billy emigrated from Vienna to the Berlin of the 1920s, a city of unbridled inflation, decadence, and a deep, varied cultural life. Earning his way as a sports and crime newsman, he frequented the coffee houses favored by filmmakers and the great galleries and museums favored by artists. In Berlin he wrote his first widely acclaimed screenplay and honed his appreciation for art. These years, prior to the rise of Hitler, shaped the budding writer-director's native talent and outlook on life. He left Berlin with both his vocation and avocation firmly in place.

Paris and New York were brief way stations en route to Wilder's inevitable destination, Hollywood. He arrived there in 1934 and opted to earn money for bread, board, and collecting as a screenwriter even though he spoke little English. Incredible as it may seem, he shortly thereafter wrote an original screen story in his newly adopted language. From then on screenplays continued without interruption, becoming the very fulcrum of his life.

Billy has had only one idol, the great German-born director Ernst Lubitsch, already a leading figure at Paramount when Wilder signed on as a very junior writer in the mid-1930s. He is proud that, with his then collaborator Charles Brackett, he wrote *Ninotchka,* a definitive Garbo film directed by Lubitsch.

Lubitsch was unique in his insistence that the words of the screenwriter be inviolate. This was, and remains today, a rare concept in an industry where the script exists to be changed. The spectacularly successful writer Larry Gelbart says of his hit play *City of Angels* that it is about a screenwriter who has "a few of his lines changed by his producer, by his director, by his secretary, by his stars, by his wife and by his mistress." Billy revered Lubitsch's point. No changes—not a word. He was rabid on the subject long before he had the contractual ability to back it up. He became a director because he was constantly angry with the mutilation of his script by other directors. He has driven actors over the wall by repeating takes where a word is missing or changed. He does not consider this nitpicking. He is deeply convinced that what is written in his office is the film.

There is no question that Billy regarded the making of a film as a constant, unremitting series of fights. His objective was unchanging. He wanted to achieve perfection. While he did not always do it, a body of work that includes *Sunset Boulevard, The Lost Weekend, Love in the Afternoon, Witness for the Prosecution, Some Like It Hot,* and *The Apartment,* made over a five-year period, would be a difficult feat for a filmmaker to surpass.

George Axelrod, author of the hit Broadway play *The Seven Year Itch,* collaborated with Billy on the screenplay. He feels that Billy was born for the medium. Most people, he says, think in words; others in pictures. Billy thinks in movies. Billy once showed Axelrod a scrap of paper which he had saved on which he had scribbled the words, *Silent picture star commits murder. When they arrest her she sees the newsreel cameras and thinks she is back in the movies*. This note had been made almost ten years before *Sunset Boulevard*.

Axelrod recalls fondly that Wilder started each day with mental warming-up exercises to prepare for the serious work ahead. One favorite form was "meet-cutes," devices whereby the leading man and the leading lady meet each other in an unusual manner. Out of hundreds, Axelrod recalls a few off the top of his head. Gary Cooper and Claudette Colbert are both in a swanky department store shopping for pajamas. He wants only the bottoms; she wants only the tops. They meet and fall in love. Another "meet-cute" involves a psychiatrist and a prostitute who both send their couches out to be recovered. The store mixes up the return deliveries. The two meet. Perhaps they fall in love.

In still another we find Audrey Hepburn in her bed, late at night, perhaps with glasses on, working a crossword puzzle. She is the wife of England's Ambassador to the United States. She picks up the telephone, calls the Russian Embassy, and asks for someone who can give her assistance. It is Yul Brynner who answers the phone. Hepburn politely asks Stalin's middle name. Brynner angrily replies, "We are not here for such nonsense." He hears Hepburn's distinctive tinkling laugh and bangs down the phone. The next night at a large ball Brynner hears that laugh. Looking up, he sees Hepburn, walks over to her and says, "Ilyich." They meet and fall in love.

Another exercise involved great openings for movies for which no plot could be found. For example, a priest is taking confession from a jockey who tells him that he is going to throw a race and begs forgiveness. His church desperately needs a new roof. The priest is torn. The next shot shows the exterior of a racetrack and features the priest on the rail with a pair of field glasses.

Another great film opening involves a *boulevardier* walking purposefully down an avenue to a point where the audience sees a sign, FENCING MASTER. He walks in and tells the master that he wants a series of lessons with the very definite purpose of becoming the finest swordsman in Paris. The teacher tells him that he cannot achieve that result since he is starting too late. The man persists, explaining that his wife is having an affair, and when he finds out who the man is he wants to

challenge him to a duel and kill him. As he is changing for the
first lesson the fencing master uses the telephone and says to
the person who answers, "Darling, he knows."

For all the fun and games, it was Billy's collaborators who
bore the brunt of his day-to-day struggle for perfection. He
took over their lives as he probed for ever better results. He
could be ruthless, insulting, never less than difficult. My beloved friend, the late Harry Kurnitz, collaborated with Billy
on a splendid screenplay, *Witness for the Prosecution*. Maurice
Zolotow's book *Billy Wilder in Hollywood* quotes Kurnitz: "His
collaborators have a hunted look, shuffle nervously and have
been known to break into tears if a door slams anywhere in
the same building. He is a fiend for work, a raving lunatic,
always saying, 'Let's make it better.' Billy at work is actually
two different people, Mr. Hyde and Mr. Hyde."

Harry, though he spoke for many others, was actually far
less disturbed by the collaborating experience. He was a world-
renowned wit, sought after on two continents to attend parties,
to be a houseguest, to have lunch, anything at all just to be
with him. I shared a home with Kurnitz for the better part of
a year and it was one of the happiest periods of my life. Furthermore, he was a great, close friend of Billy's before the
collaboration, during it, and after it. Others with a less secure
foothold took to their bed, resorted to devious methods to
avoid Wilder, or simply quit. All who survived it claim without
reservation that they learned more about picture-making during this period than from any other combination of experiences
in their career. None will ever forget the insistent clarion call,
"Let's make it better."

One of the most famous lines in the history of films was the
ending of *Some Like It Hot*. After Jack Lemmon, in drag, has
told Joe E. Brown that he cannot marry him because he is not
a woman, Brown says, "Nobody's perfect." When the time
came that the script had to be turned in, Wilder told his collaborator that they had to remember to make the last line better.
Fortunately, they never got around to it.

Billy was much harder on himself than on his collaborators.
As he searched for scenes, for lines, for phrases, for words, he
suffered to the point where he couldn't sleep and often endured
hideous back pains. Even after his reputation was secure, crit-

icism of his work was not relished. During the period when I was getting to know him he made *Ace in the Hole,* which was regarded by all critics as the height of cynicism. One day I got a call from him asking me why I was going around "knocking *Ace in the Hole.*" Stunned that he cared at all about my opinion, I responded that I felt the film was totally cynical, to which he replied, "But you must bear in mind, so am I." The prism with which he views the human condition has resulted in a brilliant career and an extraordinary series of landmark films. Like all cynics, he has, despite incessant efforts to mask it, a very soft heart indeed.

Conversely, it is not within the range of Billy's ability to allow himself to truly appreciate major honors. We lunched together the day after it was announced that he would be the 1987 recipient of the American Film Institute's Lifetime Achievement Award. It was long overdue. I was thrilled and told him so. Billy was not able to join in any celebration. He was suspicious. "I'm getting it," he said, "because Lubitsch is dead." I attended the evening, which was a monumental tribute. The next day at lunch I would brook no downplaying of this event. Anticipating his reaction, I was out of sorts as we sat down. "Billy, you can't deny it was a wonderful evening. It would be ungrateful of you not to admit it." He agreed, saying it was nice and that he was touched by Audrey Hepburn's coming halfway around the world to be with him. I was momentarily mollified until he wrapped it up by saying that any Lifetime Achievement Award was simply another marker to the grave.

He recently found in his office two messages to call Washington, a city not really on his beat. It was just at the moment when Justice William Brennan had resigned from the Bench and the press was filled with rumors about his successor. Billy immediately called Audrey and told her to pack up. "I'm being appointed to the Supreme Court," he explained. On returning the calls he found that he had been selected as a Kennedy Center Honoree for 1990. I told him I had been to many of these Award evenings and that they are wonderfully done and most prestigious. The most I could get from him was that he was happy that it did not involve moving.

He is a compulsive shopper and window-shopper, a buyer

and collector of innumerable things and objects. Although
there is no parameter to what he collects, there is generally a
lead item of the moment. Years ago a favorite was Bass Weejuns, a type of Loafer. A man who possesses six pair of Bass
Weejuns would consider himself overstocked. Wilder has
bought hundreds in his search for the perfect pair. Bass Weejuns
were preceded and followed by innumerable other items of
Billy's first choice. Shoes are an ideal example only because
they are made for walking, and in pursuing these compulsions
Wilder has walked millions of blocks, mostly in Beverly Hills,
New York, Paris, Berlin, and London. These walks are constantly interrupted by shopping, so they perhaps do not fulfill
a doctor's definition of uninterrupted exercises, which, in any
event, Wilder would resist mightily.

Shopping is an inevitable luncheon subject. He has unfailingly found something that he would like to show me. I dislike
shopping but do my best to keep my inner feelings hidden.
However, he is aware of it and complains about it. After lunch
whenever possible we go to the shop and have a look at his
item of choice. He will extol its virtues and will either urge
me to buy it or buy it for me. His generosity is enormous.

Very occasionally he will come up with a shopping suggestion on which I am as expert as he is. Not long ago, as proud
as if he had invented the electric light, he told me that he had
found a unique cashmere sweater. "Usually, you know," he
commented, "they are too heavy. These," and he uses his
fingers to show their thinness, "are very lightweight indeed.
They are the best."

These supersweaters are carried by Battaglia on Rodeo Drive
in Beverly Hills, a shop that I have been frequenting for thirty
years. Poor shopper though I am, I do know a great deal about
sweaters. Anyone who has played golf has a lot of them. If
my backswing was as good as my sweater collection I would
today be on the senior pro tour.

After lunch we advanced on Battaglia. I hoped against hope
that the sweater was new to me. The Chinese gentleman running the shop for Mr. Battaglia greeted me warmly. Wilder
asked him to show me the sweaters. When they were brought
on view he raved about them. The salesman looked quizzical
since he had long before sold me three or four. "Why don't

you," suggested Wilder, "take the yellow one? It's garish, but my feeling is that you would like it." His implied insult was correct. I did like it and bought it at a cost of two hundred and fifty dollars. I see it occasionally among my sweaters but have yet to wear it.

His shopping for food is endless. He has found a black bread which he considers superb and which his wife buys for him, but he is always looking to find a better one. Occasionally he finds a shop that he declares the winner and undisputed champion. Such a place is Sorrento's for Italian delicacies. It is a half-hour drive, but Billy goes there often. I have accompanied him on many occasions. He goes to buy specific items, but once inside the shop he is incorrigible. He looks at a very high percentage of the endless jars, tins, cans, and bottles. The proprietor leaves whoever he is with and makes the examination with him. I would guess that on a given day he might buy eighty dollars' worth of products. The proprietor, whose happiest moments are when Billy visits his emporium, gives him at least an equal amount. Often Billy will say to him, "Please give my friend every item that I have purchased and put it on my bill." I would be surprised if Billy is ever charged for this.

Nothing in the Americanization of Billy Wilder is as surprising to me as his dedication to American sports, particularly baseball. When the Dodgers first arrived in Los Angeles, he carried a portable radio with him to all dinner parties during the season. The ear attachment had not yet come into being, so at very frequent intervals he would hold his radio to his ear. He did not just limit himself to listening, but would make loud exclamations such as, "Oh, my God" and "I don't believe it." Other male guests would chorus requests about the score. If a hostess mildly rebuked him he made it clear that nothing was as important as a Dodger baseball game.

It still seems odd to me that he has such a keen understanding of the game. I am myself a rabid baseball fan and consider some of the fine points of the national pastime almost understandable. Billy, however, is very much up to speed. He prefers hearing the game on the radio to attending it or watching it on television, claiming that this method gives the mind and the imagination the greatest scope.

Pro football does not rank far behind. I was for some years part of a group of five or six men who gathered at the Wilders' to watch and bet on the Monday-night games. Our regulars included Jack Lemmon and Walter Matthau, the two actors most closely associated with Wilder films. With the exception of Matthau, we bet a hundred dollars per game against one another. Walter always had thousands of dollars at stake. The rooting of the hundred-dollar bettors was constant and loud, but the only way to learn which team Matthau was betting on was to ask him.

This custom was not all peaches and cream for Audrey. She cooked wonderful dinners, which we ate during the half. She passed excellent hors d'oeuvres which we wolfed in huge numbers, snapping them up with our eyes never leaving the television screen. She once complained bitterly to her husband that she felt she could perform this chore in the nude without anyone noticing, and she is extremely attractive. Another evening, feeling ignored, she informed Billy, "Play me or trade me." In my short and still unpublished book, "Wondrous Wives of My Friends," she is listed in the top echelon.

Billy's acerbic wit and view of life can sometimes go too far and, very often, almost too far. An example of the "almost" brand pleases me to this day. The careers of both Jack Lemmon and Walter Matthau have been immeasurably boosted by their Wilder films. Billy cares deeply about both of them, but his nature is such that he does not easily admit it.

We gave an Academy Awards party at our home in 1974. That year Jack was nominated for best actor in *Save the Tiger*. I was able to get ballots from the Academy and mailed them to our guests with instructions to fill them out and turn them in, together with fifty dollars, at the door. The one who got the most correct answers won the money. The only restriction was that everyone had to vote for Lemmon. Billy appeared with a totally uncharacteristic gesture. He opened a big bag that contained six Oscars. No one else can make precisely that contribution to an evening. He put them on a long table, three on one side and three on the other, leaving a space in the center. "Lemmon," he announced, "will walk in later and put his in the middle."

Lemmon was a surprise, long-shot winner that night. I happened to glance at Billy and saw his expression of pride, which he masked very quickly. A little later Jack came in, elated, brandishing his Oscar. He made a beeline for Billy to get the praise he wanted and deserved from the master. Wilder was at that time directing Lemmon and Matthau in a film, *The Front Page.* I happened to hear his comment to Jack. "Congratulations," he said, "but remember, don't be late to work tomorrow. Actors are apt to take these things too seriously." Lemmon was momentarily crushed. Wilder's face crinkled into a huge grin. Giving the newest Oscar winner a bear hug, he took the award and ceremoniously placed it in the middle, just as he had predicted. I immediately told Walter Matthau, who commented, "It could have gone either way."

Nothing in the busyness of his life ever stopped Billy from collecting art. It is as much a part of his life as breathing. His collecting runs as wide a gamut as his filmmaking. It has been a superb statement of the broad range of his tastes. "I have gone off in too many directions," he has said, adding philosophically, "That's just how it is. I have collected avidly."

The collection was put together over decades, slowly acquired through consistent, pleasurable effort. Los Angeles is far from a primary art center. It created for Billy greater obstacles than he would have faced if New York, London, or Paris had been his residence. He continually reads art publications and catalogs. Auctions are inexorably tracked.

Billy owns and admires greatly a stunning painting of an eye by an unknown artist. It is 17th-century French and highly symbolic of Billy Wilder, for he collects by eye—an eye that communicates instantly to his mind, his heart, and his innate, disciplined sense of quality. This permits him to judge widely diverse works of art with confidence and is the key to his becoming an important collector.

For the most part, Billy's acquisitions were made long before the artists had achieved their present reputation and price. Schwitters, the master of the small collage who only began to receive great recognition much later, was so little known in 1946 when Wilder first bought his work that the collector punned to a puzzled friend that he had decided to collect "cashmere Schwitters."

No work was purchased with a view to future value. Some naturally appreciated more than others, but to Billy this was purely a function of the marketplace, and did not affect his judgment as a collector.

Billy often buys things for a few dollars that would appear to others to have no aesthetic value at all. I was with him one day when he purchased a medium-size white Turkish towel with a bright-yellow picture of Napoleon in the center. A few weeks later I was surprised to see it simply framed and hanging with an interesting group of posters at his beach house. It was in place only for a short time, but it looked wonderful.

When it was in his home, Billy's collection was hung with a carefully planned casualness. It was no mean feat to avoid a museumlike quality to the rooms, but he brought it off. Interspersed were innumerable lamps, clocks, African and pre-Columbian sculpture, masks, and endless other objects which he still owns.

As with all true collectors, the lack of wall space is his implacable enemy. His addiction to complete sets of lithographs, particularly Stella, Hockney, and Kelly, is no help. Works of art are stacked in closets and along walls. The court of last resort is the warehouse. Billy, quite understandably, finds warehousing distasteful since it makes the art inaccessible, but he has had to do a lot of it.

Ninety-three lots were auctioned at Christie's in New York on November 13th, 1989, for a total of $32,600,000. The works included an extraordinarily disparate grouping of painters, among them Kirchner, Renoir, Rouault, Vuillard, Caillebotte, Munter, Nicholson, Braque, Miró, Hockney, Picasso, Vivin, Rimbert, Bombois, Peronnet, Botero, Balthus, Stella and Hartung. Sculptors included Marini, Manzù, Hepworth, Maillol, Calder, Giacometti, Lachaise, and Graham. The eclectic nature of the auction and Billy's name attracted a great deal of excitement. Tickets were hard to come by. Billy's guests sat in the boardroom but he was part of the crowd in the main sale room. "Not as nerve-racking as a film preview," was his judgment at the end.

Seven works sold for over one million dollars, and records were set for twelve artists. The "cashmere" Schwitters did Billy proud. Buyers obviously appreciated enormously the collection assembled over the decades by the filmmaker. That collection was removed from the Wilder apartment some six weeks before the sale. At last the annoying warehousing of art work had a major role to play.

Long before the sale, Billy's walls were filled with marvelous works of art, not of the same value as those to be auctioned but very definitely a collection that ninety-nine out of a hundred collectors would be thrilled to have as their own. Still warehoused is a large selection of paintings. The lithograph sets are still waiting their turn due to lack of space.

On the morning of December 22nd, 1989, the Wilders were rudely awakened at four A.M. Their building was on fire, so spectacularly ablaze that it was shown on national TV. Together with the other tenants, they found themselves on the street. No lives were lost, though some apartments were totally burned. The Wilder section suffered no fire, but great smoke damage. It was, to put it mildly, extraordinarily good fortune that the Christie's sale had already taken place.

It was not Wilder's first experience with fires. In 1960 he made his office at the Goldwyn Studios. He decided to make more of his collection accessible by removing many treasures from warehouses to a nearby sound stage. The temperature was ideal and there were guards on duty twenty-four hours a day. A few years later the stage was gutted by fire. It was an enormous and painful loss, which he refers to as "a traumatic weeding out."

After great inconvenience and discomfort, the Wilders are settled into a temporary apartment awaiting the day when they can return to their home. When the insurance company was cataloging his wardrobe to be sent out to have the smoke odor removed, Billy was stunned to learn that he owned sixty cashmere sweaters. Since the fire Billy has already purchased three paintings and a piece of sculpture. Long before he moves back into his own apartment he will be sending additional art objects to the warehouse.

# ME
## and
# WALTER ANNENBERG

My wife, Harriet, and Walter Annenberg's wife, Lee, are regularly told that they look and act like sisters, and indeed they do. Perhaps they picked some of it up by osmosis. For over fifty years they have been far closer than most sisters. Very few people are blessed to have a relationship of this quality weave through their lives. When they are together they cherish it. When geography is against them, which is often, they are a classic tesimonial to AT&T's insistent urging to "reach out and touch someone."

I married Harriet, and Walter Annenberg married Lee within a few months of one another some forty years ago. Both brides chafed over the fact that their brand-new husbands were total strangers. Correcting that fact was high on their agenda. That in itself posed no difficulties. Not so secretly, however, their true fantasy was to have us become instant brothers, an impossibly tall order. We were both in our late thirties. Having been to prep school and college, we were not in the marketplace desperately searching for a new best friend. Both of us, as I found out later, counseled lower expectations. It was all in vain. Nothing could shatter Lee and Harriet's illusion that Walter and I would meet one evening as strangers and part a few hours later closely bonded.

With their objective firmly in mind, they went to work on the logistics. They desired a locale providing quietness, excitement, and numerous other contradictory elements. In an amazingly short time they found a venue that filled the bill. The incomparable Judy Garland was booked to sing at the Palace Theatre in New York City at a time when we had scheduled a trip from Los Angeles. Lee and Walter would come over from Philadelphia. Since Garland performed only after the intermission, we would meet in the lobby, see her half of the show, and proceed to dinner. When the great evening arrived, our two cars approached the theatre with military precision as the intermission was drawing to a close. Walter and I shook hands, chatted for a moment in the lobby, and went on into the theatre. The first hurdle had been negotiated. We had met and not a punch had been thrown. So far so good.

It was always a thrill hearing the great Judy Garland, and afterward we adjourned to New York's famous "21" Club. Both Walter and I went there a great deal and found it an extremely comfortable setting. Not that night. Harriet and Lee were edgy and virtually twittering, making for an awkward situation. About halfway through dinner Walter put his hand on mine and said pleasantly but firmly, "Let's make it a point to get on together. It certainly is in our best interests and it will make our lives easier." Down the road I realized that I had been observing for the first time Walter's preferred way of dealing with a problem, which is to recognize it and, whenever possible, move decisively to end it. For the moment it served to break the ice and pave the way for decades of friendship with the multifaceted husband of Harriet's foster sister.

The following summer the four of us went to Europe together. I dislike and use much too often the phrase, "It's not as good as it used to be." It definitely applies, however, to European travel. In the late forties and early fifties there were not hordes of travelers. It was possible to plan a leisurely, pleasant itinerary. We did just that. We traveled well together, but did have to cope with one nagging problem on an almost daily basis. We argued regularly about the hour of dining. Harriet, Lee, and I were solidly aligned on one side; Walter, totally isolated, on the other. We wanted to make our reservations at the normal European hour. Walter, all his life a trencherman of the highest order, was constantly trying to move things earlier. We had him outnumbered, but finally one day in Paris he met us head-on. "I'm tired of being bullied around by you people," he said firmly. "I have made a seven o'clock reservation at Tour d'Argent. Everybody is entitled to have their way once in a while." Walter, it must be said, has had his way in life a great deal of the time, but he had taken enough defeats on this issue in reasonably good spirits to make further resistance futile.

We walked into Tour d'Argent, sometimes denigrated as a tourist trap but a top restaurant, promptly at seven. Busboys and waiters were finishing setting up the tables, while captains were enjoying a leisurely cigarette. We were ushered in solitary splendor to the finest table with a beautiful view of the river Seine in all its glory in bright sunlight. Walter remarked to me, "I'm glad that the Americans have finally rebelled against the insane prices that this place charges. It serves them right." Parenthetically, the absurd prices would today be the equivalent of a quick stop at McDonald's, but it was an expensive restaurant for its time.

Walter was in his glory. We had a delicious, leisurely dinner. Darkness began to descend over Paris. The city lights came on. Early arrivals began drifting into the restaurant. By the time we had finished our coffee Tour d'Argent was, as always, filled. To my discredit, I could not resist commenting to Walter as we walked out, "I notice that the Americans have forgiven Claude Terrail (the owner of Tour d'Argent) for his ridiculously high prices." Walter did not respond and it was a quiet foursome that drove back to the hotel. To his credit, he never again complained about the hour of dining throughout the rest of the trip. He chose instead to follow an adage that has occasionally served him in good stead: "There are times in life when you have to back up."

At the time of our trip to Europe television was just coming out of its infancy. There were comparatively few stations, reaching a relatively small audience. Only the most imaginative could conceive of the avalanche that would follow, changing everything in the transmission of news and entertainment. Walter, the owner of a Philadelphia station, simply took this for granted. He spoke instead of the fact that he was certain that a magazine that listed TV programs and had articles about television would have an unlimited future. We three could not see that at all. First of all, programming was offered gratis in the daily newspapers. Walter was the owner of a wide variety of publications, including the *Philadelphia Inquirer, Seventeen,* and the *Daily Racing Form*. He ran his business brilliantly. To introduce a high-risk factor of this kind into it seemed an act of folly. Our opposition seemed only to further kindle his enthusiasm. On his return to the United States he purchased three small regional TV magazines and merged them into what quickly became *TV Guide,* destined to become the flagship of his company and the largest-selling, most successful magazine in the history of publishing. It was not a bad utilization of the mind while barging around Europe for a few weeks.

Problem solving is not always as simple as it was the evening Walter and I met at the "21" Club. That night I learned that he had a pronounced stutter. He coped with it as well as possible and I simply assumed that it was a burden he would always have to accept.

As soon as we got to Europe it became apparent that nothing could be further from the truth. He was attacking the problem by doing specific speech exercises designed to eliminate it over time. The therapist who planned the program emphasized that the key to success was daily application. A day missed was a day of slippage. Walter never missed; this drill was as much a part of his routine as brushing his teeth. There was certainly no guarantee of success. Today's more precise research was not available. It was simply the best tool at hand; large doses of hope and faith were essential ingredients.

I learned the exercises very quickly. They began with a staccato, precise recitation of the vowels and included the first line of a famous British poet, Southey, "How does the water come down from Lodore?" At first I joined in, but it made him laugh and diminished his concentration. Progress was slow, but imperceptibly the stammer grew less pronounced. In 1969, when Walter was asked to be Ambassador to the Court of St. James's, there was no trace of it. He was free to accept the post, confident that the public-speaking aspect presented no hurdles.

I have naturally long since forgotten the exercises. Not so with Walter. He does them as regularly as ever. He told me recently, some forty years after I first heard them, that if he stopped, the stuttering would return within a few weeks. "Adversity," he said, "breeds discipline. That's the only way to look at it."

Some years ago I asked Walter if he had any advice for a

young New York friend of mine who had a dreadful stammer. Walter immediately told me to invite him to visit him in Philadelphia. Walter spent several uninterrupted hours teaching him the exercises and pounding away at the theme of persistence. Some time later he asked me what progress was being made. I had to regretfully report that his pupil lacked the necessary tenacity. "Too bad," Walter said. "He could have beaten it."

Over subsequent years we spent a great deal of vacation time with the Annenbergs, much of it in the Palm Springs area. They found it increasingly attractive, so it was no great surprise to us when they decided to purchase land in the area to build a winter home. I must admit that I did not even mildly conceive of what it was they were proposing to build. I do recall as though it were yesterday standing in the desert in 1962 gazing at the site that Walter, after endless study, had selected. We were looking at sand. Anyone might well have said, "Why here? Why not over there?" Needless to say, Walter had studied every aspect of the location carefully. The land was purchased in 1962 and construction began the following year. The four of us had New Year's Eve dinner together in a guest cottage in 1965 since the main house was not completed. The following year Lee and Walter took possession of their extraordinary desert home, Sunnylands. With very rare exceptions, we have spent every New Year's together at Sunnylands since that time.

Perhaps Sunnylands' greatest achievement is that, although a vast estate, it was put onto the desert floor with such taste and care that from the very beginning one felt it belonged there. In less caring hands it could have been an intrusion, but with its lush greenery, profusion of desert trees, lakes, waterfalls, and brilliantly architected home it is a desert oasis.

One feels this immediately on entering the gates and driving up the gentle manicured slope to the magnificent entrance. The house itself is grand indeed, the large rooms beautifully proportioned and gracious. The windows frame the lush acreage and golf course with the San Jacinto Mountains in the background. Perhaps frequent guests adjust, but only to a degree. Harriet and I never grow entirely used to it or take it for granted. For the first-time visitor it is overwhelming.

Sunnylands is, after all, the home of the unique Impressionist and Post-Impressionist Annenberg Collection. In addition, there is on all sides superb sculpture, art objects ranging from T'ang Dynasty tomb figures to Steuben crystal pieces. The hosts, perfectly accustomed to the reaction of their guests, are unfailingly warm and gracious. They do everything in their power to put their guests at ease, and more often than not they are successful.

Private golf courses are, to put it mildly, a rarity. The Sunnylands course is in mint condition. The fairways are lush and unscuffed. The greens, unmarred by cleat marks, are true. Since Walter prefers to play with his wife or alone, there is no need to get a starting time. I would venture to say that, even including the holiday season and weekend guests, the average number of people on the course per day over the season would be less than four.

Playing there as I have so many times, often alone, is a great privilege. For a golf aficionado it should be the equivalent of paradise. It has, however, one major drawback. All the numerous excuses for hitting bad shots are summarily removed. There are no players behind you crowding you. No one is hitting into you. Errant balls from other fairways do not land close to you, lessening your concentration. The dread cry of FORE! is never heard. The truth is that all the blame for bad shots falls on the shoulders of that most vulnerable of species, the player, and there are plenty of opportunities for bad shots.

Walter is a keen lover of trees. Every species that blooms in the desert can be found on the course. I have, at one time or another, hit them all, which gives me the dubious distinction of having hit every type of desert tree.

On most desert courses if one hits the ball in front of the green it will roll on. The Sunnylands greens are on undulant rises guarded by tall (perhaps too tall) grass, so there is no alternative but to hit the ball onto the green.

Water is perhaps the single element that contributes most to the beauty of Sunnylands, but on a round where I hit two or three balls into the water I am not as appreciative of this fact as I should be.

If ever there was a man who can fully appreciate a private

golf course, Walter is that man. He loves the game, but his agenda is different from most golfers'. He does not regard eighteen holes with three other sociable folks as the sport's primary purpose. Betting holds no lure for him. Walter loves the essential thing about golf, which is hitting the ball. Poor shots do not bother him since he expects them; he gets full pleasure out of good shots. His mind is on his game, but at the same time it roams over other facets of his life. He is an inveterate bird watcher. He carries a pair of binoculars with him and automatically picks up a secondary pleasure on the course.

For a period of several years when he underwent hip operations he could not play at all. He never complained, remaining confident that he would get back to the game. So he has, with a backswing that is greatly improved. Many years ago the two of us took lessons from a lady professional who called him "Zorro," claiming he had "the fastest swing in the West." She could not say that today. The only facet of my own game that I think has improved is my disposition. Walter had many occasions to remind me of the late TV host and columnist Ed Sullivan's advice, "Golf is a game of ease, not an easy game."

In 1969 President Nixon offered Walter the prestigious post of Ambassador to the Court of St. James's. Walter accepted and served for five years. He and Lee, initially total novices in the diplomatic sector, hit their stride early on. They were a remarkably successful team. To a degree, ambassadorships are what the individual chooses to make them. Walter elected to work very hard indeed. His greatest adjustment was that in private life he was the boss. His decisions were final and speedily implemented. In London, representing the views of his Government, he reported to the Secretary of State. It made for a slower pace, but playing a vital role in so many important matters was a compensating satisfaction. His duties, including many others, ran the gamut of working with the Prime Minister, the Secretary of Foreign and Commonwealth Affairs, and other key Government figures, knowing British leaders and opinion makers from the private sector, representing American private interests when appropriate, maintaining friendly relationships with other ambassadors, and hosting innumerable official and unofficial delegations and visitors from the United States.

Much of it was official Embassy business, but endless social engagements were essential to make the wheels go around. Lee, a brilliant hostess, was indefatigable. Receptions, lunches, and dinners at Winfield House, the beautiful United States Embassy Residence, were superb. This facet of their diplomatic life was a hallmark of their English experiences.

Although their calendars were overcrowded, their hospitality to us started early on and was unceasing. During our visits to Winfield House we had the opportunity to share with them many grand events. Oddly enough, it is a few of the more intimate remembrances, spread over the years, that remain particularly meaningful.

One Saturday afternoon during an early visit we went with Lee and Walter to the Tate Gallery, where some thirty paintings from the Annenberg Collection were on view. Although regularly exposed to these works of art, I must admit I had not quite realized their number and importance. The reviews had been brilliant. The crowd was large. Walter, thoroughly enjoying his anonymity, chatted with other viewers as we made our way along. We capped it off with high tea at one of the hotels. Particularly in view of experiences that lay ahead in this area, it was a wonderful afternoon.

Another time we took a granddaughter, Janet Granger, then twelve or thirteen, on what I call a "Changing of the Guard, Eiffel Tower" trip to Europe. On our second evening in London the Alvin Ailey Dance Company was performing under the joint sponsorship of the Duke and Duchess of Kent and Lee and Walter. We three were invited to sit in the VIP loge circle. During intermission we were ushered to the manager's small office for refreshments. There was the normal shaking of hands all around. Janet, looking solemnly at each person, repeated, "I am glad to meet you." The formality of her demeanor must have amused the Duke, who, with equal solemnity, bowed and responded, "And I am pleased to meet you." Walter, who chanced to view the incident, murmured to me, "That's an extremely cordial greeting between two people neither of whom has a clue as to who the other person is." It began our trip on a higher note than Janet realized.

A visit to Winfield House happened to coincide with the Wimbledon Tennis Tournament. Lee and Walter, as always, gave us a warm, welcoming dinner. In his remarks Walter expressed regret that because of a lapse of memory the best of his ticket allocations had been given out. Our seats were not as good as he would have wished, but he knew I would forgive him. In my response I said that Harriet and I were touched by his toast but, as an avid tennis fan, it was premature to issue forgiveness. There was a general murmur of approval around the table. By the time the evening was over I was the proud possessor of enough excellent Wimbledon seats to become a ticket scalper.

On occasion Walter saw an opportunity to perform a unique service for Great Britain. When that happened he seized upon it. He learned early on that, inexplicably, there was no definitive book on Westminster Abbey. Feeling the need for such a volume, he set about producing it. The result is a landmark 250-page volume, *Westminster Abbey,* that came off the press in 1972. The photographs and maps, which are superb, are more than matched by the brilliant texts supplied by Britain's finest historians and scholars. This volume was disseminated widely not only to the Abbey but to colleges, universities, and libraries. It will, I am certain, stand any test of time as the authoritative work on the subject.

After five years Walter was understandably eager to return to private life. President Ford urged him to stay on, but he submitted his resignation and returned home in late 1974. For Lee it had been a highlight that for a time she actively missed. Not so with Walter. Although he treasured the memories of his experiences, he returned to his business, his other activities, Philadelphia, and particularly to Sunnylands, with gusto.

There are still steady visitations to Sunnylands from Great Britain, including members of the Royal Family, top Government officials past and present, and many friends. Walter maintains a warm, broadly based correspondence. When they return to England they are warmly received. Walter believes that when it's over it's over and these visits are not too frequent.

In 1976 he was awarded an honorary KBE, Knight of the British Empire, the only United States Ambassador to be so honored and a splendid validation of his tenure. He did not for one instant miss his stride in returning to an early dinner hour, a habit that had not jibed with his ambassadorial duties.

In 1975 Lee and Walter invited to Sunnylands four Southern California couples, all close friends, as their houseguests for their three-day New Year's celebration. This group, made up of the Ronald Reagans, William Wilsons, Earle Jorgensens, and William French Smiths, were soon joined by a Kansas City couple, Charles and Carol Price, and has continued without interruption. It happened at a moment in our lives when we were becoming increasingly aware of the importance and value of longtime friendships. The years shared with these gifted hosts so close to all of us have only enhanced this feeling.

There is golf, tennis, and good conversation, combined with lunches and dinners and a fair share of football Bowl-watching on New Year's Day.

The high point is the stunning New Year's Eve party of approximately eighty guests, meticulously planned by Lee. It is a particularly cherished event, and sharing it for the eight Reagan years with the President of the United States and Nancy gave it an added dimension.

Ever since I met Walter, except for his London years, his stewardship of his company was inextricably tied to his life. A few years ago when he sold the company I could not help but wonder if he would miss it and the responsibilities that went with it. My concern was wasted. His other interests, particularly philanthropy, jumped to the foreground and he seems busier than ever.

Walter is regularly involved in highly personalized one-on-one philanthropy, often triggered by an obvious injustice. The beneficiary may well be someone he has never met and will never meet.

Some years ago Harriet and I were at Sunnylands for a quiet weekend. On a beautiful Sunday morning I went to Walter's office for coffee, to be followed by nine holes of golf. In an office closet he has an AP printer which clatters off fast-breaking news. It has been some years since Walter was an active publisher, but this is a reading habit he does not choose to break. As I walked in he was reading the latest printout. It was obvious that he was in a fury. "Look at this," he said, handing it to me. "This is a damned outrage." The item involved the Houston widow of a soldier killed in Vietnam who was being evicted from her home for falling behind on her mortgage payments.

Walter instantly called his lawyer in Philadelphia. In my mind's eye I saw this worthy sharing a cold Philadelphia Sunday with his wife. Walter's anger rose a notch as he posted the lawyer on what he had just read. He said, "I think the way to cope with this is for you to fly down to Houston immediately, pay the mortgage off tomorrow, and clear the problem up. Make very certain of our anonymity." We went out for our golf game, followed by lunch with our wives.

A few days later, talking to Walter from Los Angeles, I asked him if the Houston matter had been settled. At first he truly did not recall what I meant. When I reminded him he said, "Oh, yes, the widow now owns her home outright."

All of us dream the impossible dream of waving a magic wand and righting an impossible wrong. Few can do it. It would require a major research project to uncover how many of the few who can do it do do it.

Walter's philanthropies are innumerable. To me the most fascinating, complex example is the Annenberg Schools for Communication since they are a direct result of Walter's life-long experience in this field. Although there are offshoots, the two main schools are at the University of Pennsylvania, launched in 1958, and the University of Southern California, launched in 1971.

We are an information-based society. As everything to do with communications becomes more complex, these schools, with their extensive libraries and computing systems, are a base for contributing leadership and excellence into this vast, complex area.

Books and articles constantly present new research in the field; conferences and workshops result in the dissemination of further knowledge. Television broadcasts of the highest order emanate from the schools. The most important components are the splendid faculty and the hundreds of graduates with advanced degrees who go on to play a vital leadership role in all branches of communication. The funding of the buildings, the programs, and the curricula over the years compose an enormous contribution to a field which stands at the core of our lives.

The scope, diversity, and philosophy involving Walter's charities should one day be the subject of a book on the art of philanthropy.

Among Walter's many achievements, the assemblage of the Annenberg Collection must be considered the crown jewel. The first acquisitions were made in the 1950s. I feel certain that neither Lee nor Walter could have foretold that the end result would be one of the greatest privately held Impressionist and Post-Impressionist collections. By 1980 every great artist of the period was represented. In 1983 Walter made a quantum leap by adding fifteen works from the collection of his sister, Enid Haupt. The hallmark of the Annenberg Collection is, I am told, that every picture comprising it is of museum quality. To see it come into being and grow to its present greatness has been a rich dividend.

Several years ago Lee and Walter decided to exhibit their collection. They chose to show it initially at the Philadelphia Museum of Art in the summer of 1989. Since they happened to be in Los Angeles, Harriet and I flew with them for the opening evening. I was unprepared for the vast difference between seeing the art at Sunnylands and in a museum setting. Both venues are remarkable but, perhaps because I was so accustomed to seeing the home installation, the museum view permitted me to see it from a new perspective.

During the first half of the summer of 1990 the collection graced Washington's National Gallery of Art. During the second half it was on display at the Los Angeles County Museum of Art. I did not see the Washington exhibition, but was filled with parochial pride at the Los Angeles opening. The installation was superb. It is, incidentally, completely impossible, no matter how directly or obliquely one tries, to extract a viewpoint, to get even a hint of a comment from either Lee or Walter on the comparative installations, but they are both gratified at the huge number of viewers that have attended all three. The summer of 1991 will find the Annenberg Collection at the Metropolitan Museum of Art in New York.

Since this may be one of the very last great collections that might be given to a museum, it is not surprising that I am often asked about its destination. The questioners, often interested partisans, are generally disappointed by my truthful answer, "I don't know." I am no longer surprised by the follow-on question, asking if I have a clue as to whether Lee and Walter have reached a decision. The same answer applies, but I sometimes give it emphasis by saying, "I don't have a clue." I then volunteer the information that it is a matter to which Walter gives continuing thought and suggest that he might be the perfect person to ask. This invariably brings the discussion to an end.

I treasure the diversity of subjects Walter and I have discussed over the years. The term "long-range" invariably is part of the base of his thinking process. Our friendship has long ago passed that test. We are still, and always will be, outranked by our wives, but we two have traveled a long, satisfying road since that first dinner at "21."

# ME

*and*

# THE BARRYMORES

"COULD YOU PLEASE come up to my office as soon as possible."
I received that telephone call in 1953, but it is still vividly
implanted in my memory. I was enjoying the splendid life of
a Metro-Goldwyn-Mayer contract producer. The call came
from Benjamin Thau, a top studio executive.

Today, most independent film producers lead an existence
that appears scientifically designed to produce not films, but
heart attacks, ulcers, night sweats, and anxiety attacks. Our
lives were placid by comparison. The studio was totally self-
contained with producers, stars, directors, and writers plus
every department and craft to take a film from inception into
the theatres. A certain amount of intramural fighting naturally
went on, but compared to today it was a placid millpond.
Material was shoved at us in profusion. We were encouraged
to submit projects to the studio. Our basic chore was to guide
two or three films annually through the mill. There was a great
deal of work involved, but none that produced a deterioration
of health.

There was only one seemingly insignificant fly in that wonderful ointment. The top-echelon producers got first crack at
all the goodies. Those of us ranked in the second or third
echelon got what was left. For a long time I received fine
material and had no trouble handling my quota. A point arrived, however, when six or eight months had gone by without
my finding anything I liked. I had no film in production, no
scripts in writing, a situation which the studio would not tol-
erate. That, I suspected, was the reason for Ben Thau's telephone call.

I was not too alarmed, since we were good friends. When
I arrived at MGM, my friend and mentor, Dore Schary, urged

me to cultivate these men since there was bound to be some resentment about the easy way I slid in the MGM door through Schary, who was the new head of production.

Ben and I hit it off well. We reached the point where every few weeks I would have dinner with him and Spencer Tracy at Romanoff's, a famous restaurant of the day. At first I looked forward to these dinners. Tracy was an enormous star, and I assumed they would be interesting. In point of fact, they very rarely spoke. It was almost as if they were members of an order of priests who had taken a vow of silence. I persevered, however, remembering Schary's admonition.

From the moment I entered his office I realized that there was nothing sociable about this meeting. After courteously telling me to sit down, he said pleasantly, "You're falling behind here. I'm sure you are aware of that." "I know it," I replied heatedly, "because you are constantly giving everything that is any good to a handful of producers. By the way, how do you get into that group?" "You get into it," he said quietly, "by making a series of good pictures and hoping that one of them catches fire."

He then went on to say that, as I was aware, in a situation of this sort, the studio assigned a project to the dilatory producer. When I asked what he had in mind for me, he said, "You are going to produce a film entitled *Kind Lady* starring Ethel Barrymore."

I was aware that Miss Barrymore was under contract to the studio. She was, of course, an integral part of the royal American theatre family, The Barrymores. For years they had dominated Broadway and American stages with enormously popular and often bravura performances. Not until Alfred Lunt and Lynn Fontanne appeared on the scene much later was their family supremacy ever challenged. I, for one, never thought the Lunts came close to unseating them. Although a great stage star, Miss Barrymore had never made a mark in films. MGM, feeling for some strange reason that they could find juicy roles for her, gave her a splendid contract. For them it was an error in judgment. For her it was manna from heaven. It kept her from finishing her life in not-too-genteel poverty.

It never occurred to her that she should be treated in any

way but as a star. Oddly enough, no one at the studio, from Louis B. Mayer down, had the courage to tell her otherwise. Consequently, she had a dressing room comparable to the likes of Elizabeth Taylor's and Ava Gardner's, and all the other perks including a limo and driver to take her to and from the set. The only problem was that she never needed to be taken to and from the set. She never worked.

I had seen the melodrama *Kind Lady* on the New York stage. It was a quite compelling story about an old lady in a wheelchair who, for reasons not altogether clear to me then or now, was held captive in her own home by unscrupulous people, headed by the villain, whose job it was to see that she was totally isolated. I could not, in my wildest dreams, conceive of transposing this extremely confined material to the screen.

I was incredulous. I said, "Ben, this place is filled with stars, most of whom are not working. Why are you doing this to me? Why are you doing it at all? You are proposing to make a movie starring Ethel Barrymore that no one will go to see." "Well," he explained calmly, "we have had three or four scripts written and rewritten for her, plus the fact that we have a considerable amount of money tied up in her back salary with nothing to show for any of it. She certainly is not getting any younger. Also, the accounting department has advised us that it would be cheaper to make the film and write it off."

By now I was angry and said, "The accounting department, with your help, is also writing me off. Once this project is finished, I will be out on the street and you will still be sitting behind that big desk." He ended the meeting by saying, "It's not that serious. We all know that these things happen. We can't have the year go by with your having made only one picture. Then you *would* be out on the street. You take these scripts home and read them tonight. They're not too bad. We'll get together tomorrow." I left with the scripts under my arm, certain that the MGM caper was over for me. Nothing I read that night changed my mind, but I did have a harrowing thought.

Twelve years earlier, through pull and good fortune, I was hired as assistant talent buyer for the Rudy Vallee radio program emanating from New York. There was no television.

Vallee was popular. The ratings were high. It was a fun job. Just as it was decided to move the show to Los Angeles for a few months, the head talent buyer became ill. With less than six months of experience I inherited his job. For the most part it was simple enough since the talent agents were eager to get their clients on the show.

Inevitably, the week came along when we could not land anybody. In desperation we signed John Barrymore, erstwhile great Shakespearean actor and the most famous of the Barrymore clan. We knew he was well past his prime and had a drinking problem. Still, we were totally unprepared when he appeared for rehearsal. He was a wreck. Helped to the stage by a small retinue, he was unkempt and disheveled. To say that he was drunk was to say that it drizzled at the Johnstown flood. The Great Profile, world famous for so long, was in tatters.

Not so, as we quickly learned, the equally renowned voice. It miraculously remained vibrant and compelling. We got through the rehearsal and he returned for the show only slightly more drunk than he had been. An excellent pseudo-Shakespearean role had been written for him. He did it comedically and well. We heaved a collective sigh at having dodged a very live bullet, happy that we would never have to go through that again. We were wrong. The mail tripled, the ratings rose. The powers that be, all safely ensconced in the East, insisted despite our violent protests that we sign this hulk for eight weeks.

In the twinkling of an eye my job deteriorated from talent buyer to Barrymore's keeper. Three days before each show I would go to his house, hoping against hope to find him somewhat sober. It never happened. The house, which had obviously been grand in some past time, was musty and dank. Under any and all conditions, men like John Barrymore manage to retain some camp followers. How he paid them I had no idea. Half seemed fiercely devoted to keeping liquor from him while the other half fought to supply him with it. They were the steady winners.

During this degrading period, I observed his tantrums, his unconfined bathroom habits, his abstinence from the shower, and other endearing traits. I often helped him pull his trousers on over his swollen ankles so that we could shove him into a car for the journey to NBC.

Each broadcast was a trauma. His language was constantly vile. If used on the air, it would close down the program and perhaps even the network. The urge to escape destitution is a strong one. Some inner mechanism kept him in check while on the air. At the end of the eight weeks they actually wanted to renew him but were reluctantly convinced that the risk was not acceptable.

While preparing for *Kind Lady*, it did not escape me that Lionel Barrymore had played a supporting role in *Right Cross*, a film I had recently produced starring June Allyson and Ricardo Montalban. Lionel, having overcome his drug problem, caused me no trouble, but it seemed to me an unfortunate coincidence that his health permitted him no choice but to play his role in a wheelchair and that Ethel Barrymore for this role would also be confined to a wheelchair. Not a happy omen. In my melancholy I became convinced that this famous family harbored some resentment against me and was determined to bring me to my knees.

The next morning I went into Ben Thau's office, reconciled to the inevitable. I reasoned I should have been more industrious and not allowed myself to get to this point. I did have one glimmering hope. "Ben," I said, "at least see if you can borrow Ray Milland from Paramount to play the villain who imprisons Miss Barrymore." "That is impossible," he said. "We also owe a picture to Maurice Evans and he is going to play that part."

Evans was a fine British Shakespearean actor who had occasionally appeared on the New York stage. The most exhaustive poll would not have unearthed more than a few hundred people in America who had ever heard of him. This was the last straw. I said firmly, "Rather than have this happen to me, I'll take a suspension." His reply was a classic example of the studio mentality. "You can't take a suspension," he said. "You don't make enough money." This, by the way, was in 1953. I was getting over $1,000 per week, not too bad for someone who three years earlier had never seen the inside of a motion picture studio. In fact, when I first learned my salary I called my office in New York to tell them never to buy any motion picture stocks since these people were all crazy.

Maurice Evans was hurtling with all possible speed on the 20th Century Limited and the Super Chief, ready to report so that this disaster could get under way. Miss Barrymore was presumably in her splendid dressing room eagerly awaiting instructions. John Sturges, whom I liked and with whom I had worked before, was assigned to the picture. Pre-production work began immediately. This part of filmmaking can be elaborate and time consuming. Such was not the case with *Kind Lady*. Virtually the entire melodrama was played with Miss Barrymore in a wheelchair, confined to the house in which she was held prisoner.

To my regret, nothing horrible happened to Maurice Evans. He arrived in my office on schedule, a mild, pleasant, neutral-looking Englishman. I naturally addressed him as Mr. Evans. He insisted that I call him Morris. "That," I said, "seems extremely familiar. What is the matter with Maurice?" He replied that Maurice was indeed his given name, but that his friends all called him Morris. My pleasure in having found a new friend was far outweighed by the fact that he was definitely a member in good standing of the English stage tradition of mumblers.

Decades later Rex Harrison, when asked why he never attempted Shakespeare, replied that for the most part Shakespearean actors mumbled or shouted their lines. He therefore avoided the Bard. Not so with Morris. Sturges and I fervently hoped that the studio's excellent sound department could turn what he said into something that would be at least partially understood by an individual with average hearing, should any such person ever stumble into the theatre.

During this period I regularly called on Miss Barrymore. In fact, the wardrobe department and everyone else connected with the film came by common consent to see her. This fascinated me because she was perfectly capable of making the usual rounds. She never asked for special treatment, it just came her way. The famous Barrymore profile, her piercing blue eyes, stunning gray hair, and regal presence made all hands eager to pay her that homage.

Once, just once, I was ten minutes late for an appointment in her dressing room. She was very angry. I told her the time had gotten away from me, but she was slow to forgive. She was a casual friend of my mother's. At one point in her harangue she told me that she would tell my mother about my rudeness. Since I was deep in my thirties, I could not help but smile. I begged, "Please, Miss Barrymore, for God's sake don't tell my mother." On that note we made our peace.

The roster of players under contract to the studio was so large that some of them went virtually unnoticed. The part of the maid, evil incarnate under Morris' thumb, was played by Angela Lansbury, who later went on to bigger and better things.

Inevitably, shooting began with Miss Barrymore firmly ensconced in her wheelchair, while the rest of the cast went to incredible lengths to isolate her. Each evening, Sturges and I looked at the dailies. Miss Barrymore did not condescend to appear. I doubt that Morris was even aware of the procedure. To our benumbed senses it seemed to be going along, as a doctor might say to the offspring of a critically ill parent, "as well as can be expected."

Happily we stayed on schedule and on budget. We had naturally assumed that Miss Barrymore would require endless retakes. We were wrong. Each day she had her lines down cold and was sharp as a tack. The dreaded call from the front office criticizing our efforts never came through. A moment finally arrived when I figured that this, too, would pass. I began to industriously search for other projects to prevent this from ever happening to me again.

My comparative euphoria did not last long. Miss Barrymore, no longer young and long a toper in the Barrymore tradition, developed a pronounced wheeze in her voice. When she hit the letter $s$ it sounded like a train whistle.

In a tight little melodrama everything has to work perfectly if it is to work at all. Her voice now made the proceedings funnier than Abbott and Costello. The rushes spoke, or whistled, for themselves. The soundmen told us they could not contain the problem. The hissing film would have to be reshot. It was obvious that we would have to shut down until our leading lady recovered. Shutting down involved problems including added costs. I had enough malice in my heart not to be too upset.

Production head Dore Schary was out of town, so I dealt directly with the MGM czar, Louis B. Mayer. Together we would see the film. His official announcement would follow.

We sat together in the dark as Miss Barrymore's bronchial condition filled the projection room. The moment the lights came up, he grabbed my arm like a sumo wrestler. Eyes blazing, he pronounced, "Go ahead as fast as you can. She will be dead in six weeks and we'll be stuck with all that film."

Like the Supreme Court, there is no appeal. We did as ordered. As comedian Joe E. Lewis once said, "I'm not drinking any more. Of course I'm also not drinking any less." So it was with Miss Barrymore. She did not get any worse. Of course, she did not get any better. The final shot was finally in the can. Miss Barrymore outlived Mayer's prediction, but she never worked again. Those fly-by-the-seat-of-their-pants gambling film-industry pioneers did not achieve their place in the sun without reason.

No wrap party marked the conclusion of the filming of *Kind Lady*, but Sturges and I got quite drunk in my office. What we had to show for our efforts were some cans of film that we prayed were usable. It never occurred to us to hope for more than that.

Experts worked endlessly on the sound track until Miss Barrymore's wheezes and sibilant *s*'s were virtually nonexistent. Only Evans' mumbling remained. Nothing could be done about that.

The balance of the post-production work, which usually takes forever, proceeded with what seemed to me blinding speed.

The inevitable day came when *Kind Lady* was ready for its first preview. I was among those present. It is bad form to miss your own hanging. I had already mentally packed my personal office belongings and was beginning to miss my grand suite with its private bathroom. I expected the audience to roar with laughter, walk out, do everything short of pelting the screen. It slowly dawned on me that these misguided souls, while not ecstatic, were going along with the movie. The preview cards they filled out on leaving the theatre furnished

additional proof; perhaps, just perhaps, I had received a re-
prieve from the Governor. The studio brass were strangely
docile. After all, the movie had been made and written off.
Following a few minor changes, the film was shipped to New
York to be viewed by the real bosses, the heads of Loew's,
Inc., the owners of MGM.

There was an old saying at the studio that many films, like
fine wines, did not travel well. Judged excellent on leaving
California, they were viewed with a jaundiced eye on their
New York arrival. Not so with *Kind Lady*. Nicholas Schenck,
Loew's Chairman and well into his seventies, loved it. He
congratulated all concerned, including me. We had, he pronounced, a fine motion picture on our hands that should do
good business and be a credit to the studio. I heard all this in
the same dazed condition I had been in since the assignment
was first thrust on me.

Considerable money was spent promoting *Kind Lady*. I was
flown to New York for press interviews and heard my forked
tongue proclaim that from the start I had believed wholeheartedly in the project. My pre-judged nightmare actually opened
at Radio City Music Hall, the showcase of the day, to admiring,
respectful reviews. It quickly established its identity as an example of moderate-budget, quality filmmaking. By the time
I returned to California I was taking modest bows and, in a
self-deprecating way, explaining that filming in such confined
sets was no mean feat. I was on the verge of regarding myself
as an excellent producer of melodrama until, a year later, I saw
*Rear Window* and found out what a rattling, nail-biting, ten-
sion-packed film can be made in very confined space. I remained philosophical.

In a 1988 Vice Presidential debate, Senator Quayle compared
his congressional experience with that of John F. Kennedy.
Senator Bentsen replied eloquently that Quayle was "no Jack
Kennedy." Well, Miss Barrymore was no Grace Kelly. Maurice Evans was no James Stewart. John Sturges and I together
were no Alfred Hitchcock. Ergo, *Kind Lady* was no *Rear Window*. In a comparative sense, it could be said that we fared
better. They expected a hit; they got it. We expected a train
wreck; we avoided it.

They were brilliant stars, but as pointed out in Margot Peters' recent Barrymore biography, all were stalemated from achieving their full potential by a lack of discipline and a recurrent urge toward self-destruction.

Hardly a man is now alive who worked with all three of them. *The Guinness Book of Records* is probably waiting eagerly for me to step forward.

# ME

*and*

# NANCY REAGAN

LITTLE GIRLS by the tens of millions dream of becoming actresses. The glamour, the excitement, the applause, the goddesslike quality have an irresistible lure. As Maurice Chevalier so wisely tells us in *Gigi*, little girls get bigger every day. By the time this inevitable occurrence has taken place, most of them, for various reasons, have abandoned all hope for an acting career. They are the fortunate ones. The tiny majority who persist face the chanciest life imaginable. Only a handful get as high as the first rung of the ladder. Those that do climb higher do not, with rare exceptions, find it a fortunate calling. It is chaotic and filled to overflowing with disappointments. Some of the glamour remains, but it is certainly not on the front burner.

In the golden days of Hollywood the studio contract system provided a relatively safe haven for a chosen few. They received that rarest of commodities, a weekly paycheck. If their films led to any degree of public acceptance, the studios tried extremely hard to move their careers forward. I would hazard a guess that for most of these actresses their years under contract would rank as the brightest part of their professional lives.

Of all the studios that flourished during that era, MGM had the longest list of contract players. The longevity of a studio career was not as great as one might think, because it was heavily weighted by a few at the top. The Elizabeth Taylors and the Ava Gardners stayed under contract for a long time. However, as one went down the scale in importance and salary, the names and numbers of the players changed quite rapidly. Newcomers were always a threat, parts became fewer, and eventually the contract was not renewed. Some, Debbie Reynolds for example, had the talent to press forward with a long, successful career. Angela Lansbury simply marked time at MGM and only later realized her potential. Katharine Hepburn, Greta Garbo, and Elizabeth Taylor established themselves as lifetime stars. The majority faded out of the business within a handful of years.

When I was producing films at MGM in the early 1950s there were perhaps thirty-five actresses under contract. If anyone had suggested that this group would include a future princess and a future first lady, that person, although later judged clairvoyant, would have been mercifully bundled off to a psychiatrist by a caring friend. The list, however, did include Grace Kelly and Nancy Davis, later to become better known as Nancy Reagan. Grace Kelly was a star; Nancy Davis was a successful supporting actress. The two became and remained good friends for the rest of Grace's life, often referring to themselves as MGM graduates.

I produced a film, *Green Fire*, in which Grace costarred with Stewart Granger. I had not met her, so some weeks prior to filming, her agent brought her to my office. She was not yet the star she would soon become, but all the portents were there. She looked, as all the world would quickly come to know, cool and beautiful. Granger, one of my favorite gin rummy opponents, was lounging on my office sofa and also met her for the first time. The agent proudly showed us a picture of his budding star on the cover of an upcoming issue of *Life* magazine. I said, "Grace, what a wonderful cover. You look marvelous." Granger, eager to protect his star turf, quickly volunteered that he had also "had" the *Life* cover. She responded pleasantly, "I am sure you have, but I'm just starting, and feel so lucky to get this break right away." It was a splendid put-down that somehow made the handsome swashbuckler seem a trifle older. The film was certainly not one of Grace Kelly's finest, although it was well received and profitable. Most of it was shot in Bogotá, Colombia, which in that pre-drug era seemed to all of us a pleasant, hospitable location.

A few years later, when word spread through the studio that Grace was giving all this up to marry Prince Rainier of Monaco, there were many who doubted the wisdom of her choice. Who in their right mind, they wondered, would give up being a queen in films to be a princess in Monaco? An MGM producer said to her at one of several going-away parties, "Why are you doing this? Our back lot is many times larger than Monaco, and we have almost as much gambling at the studio as they have in that entire country." Perhaps it was the word "serene" that tilted her in the direction she took. She was, after all, destined to be Her Serene Highness Princess Grace of Monaco. Had she opted for a different course, the word "serene" would rarely have entered her life no matter how high she had risen in the ranks of motion picture royalty.

Nancy Davis came to MGM in 1949, about a year after my arrival. She had headed for Broadway on her graduation from Smith. Her mother, who had had a long acting career, is the one who nurtured the idea. Nancy did some summer stock, played in several road company productions, and appeared in a Broadway hit, *Lute Song*, starring Mary Martin and Yul Brynner. In the time-honored tradition, someone saw her work, liked it, and arranged for her to have a screen test at MGM.

I did not know of her existence until I received a memo on my desk from the front office to all producers which read: "There is a screen test of NANCY DAVIS in projection room C. Please look at it promptly and let us know your opinion." Since the studio was constantly on the prowl for new talent, these memos were frequent occurrences. The formula never varied. A scene was selected. The individual being tested did part of it full-face and part from either profile. They were directed by young men just starting out; the day of the female director was a long way off.

When I saw this test I was startled to note on the slate that it was directed by George Cukor, one of the most prominent directors in the history of MGM. He was certainly never asked to direct screen tests. Many of the producers, a cynical group, could not resist writing in their reports, "The girl looks fine, but I recommend you try to sign the director." With all that, the reaction to Nancy was positive, and so it was that the attractive girl with big brown eyes signed on at MGM. Some time later I learned that it was Spencer Tracy, a longtime friend of Nancy's parents, who prevailed upon Cukor to do the test.

Nancy and I soon met one another. She was euphoric about her weekly paycheck and the fairyland studio atmosphere. The MGM commissary, with the likes of Fred Astaire, Lana Turner, June Allyson, Judy Garland, Elizabeth Taylor, Deborah Kerr, Esther Williams, Robert Taylor, Van Johnson, Gene Kelly, and Frank Sinatra, seemed unreal. With all of that, it made a newcomer feel more than a little nervous.

I walked into the commissary one day just as Nancy came in. On the spur of the moment, I invited her to lunch. This was rarely done. The commissary, albeit glamorous, was the company restaurant to which people went in the normal course of their business day. It was commonly accepted that everyone paid for their own lunch. I decided to be a big-time sport because I had already learned that we were both Chicagoans, and she did appear quite alone.

To my horror, she ordered a steak, stewed tomatoes, spinach, and a piece of melon. Within the twinkling of an eye she had built up a check of at least five dollars, gigantic in the currency of the day, especially since the commissary was not run for profit. I told her in no uncertain terms that she should never count on my taking her to lunch again. It was the first time I ever heard her unique, infectious, wonderful laugh. Far more important, it was the very beginning of a friendship that has lasted over forty years and is still going strong.

We ran into one another at the studio. I often hosted Sunday-buffet lunches of the "drop over if you feel like it" variety. Nancy sometimes came over for lunch and swimming. From time to time hostesses asked me to escort her to dinner parties. At one of these parties I happened to look her directly in the eye and made a slight facial expression that I assume combined disdain and boredom. I was startled when her eyes widened and she began, for no discernible reason, to laugh. I completed my new act by briefly putting my finger to my lips as though to hush up an unruly child. She simply could not stop laughing and finally had to take out a handkerchief to wipe the tears from her eyes. When asked what it was all about, she pointed to me and said, "It's him." I defended myself stoutly, saying that I had done nothing, but a Svengali-like pattern had been started which I found irresistible.

One day Louis B. Mayer called a meeting of all hands on a large sound stage. I was only a few seats away from Nancy. As soon as our leader was well into his harangue, warning us that we must all be alert to the threat of Communism at the studio, I leaned over and whispered to her, "If you laugh now it could cost you your job." She, incredulous, answered, "Why would I laugh?" It was the cue for my facial expression, but I mercifully turned away. It finally reached a point when a raised eyebrow did the trick. It was too easy, so I stopped. Years later I tried it once more for old time's sake, but she had developed an immunity. A withering look was her only response.

Nancy's career was, by any standards, a success. Few actresses who decide to try for the brass ring rise as high. She appeared in a dozen films, receiving star billing in several. Her niche was the girl on the next street, à la June Allyson, as opposed to the girl on the next planet, à la Joan Crawford. It was a happy period in her life, but all of it was a prelude to her meeting Ronnie Reagan in 1950. Being a wife had always rated far higher on her priority list, so when they married in 1952 that phase of her life ended with no regrets.

I had known Ronnie casually for some time. One incident that I had heard about him stood out above all others, marking him as far more than another film personality.

While at Warner Bros. he belonged to an excellent golf club that had the virtue of being close to the studio. He enjoyed it and loved the game. Once, in his ignorance, he proposed a Jewish friend for membership. The action was scoffed at and derided. When the name was posted, as required, some members threw darts at it. Ronnie took the paper down and put it in his card case. He showed it often through the years to people as he expressed his outrage. He resigned immediately. I had the opportunity of learning early on that he is a man of strong, steadfast views.

His views on abortion and gun control, both of which I disagree with, were equally immovable. Early in his first campaign for the Presidency I went to his home to urge him to reconsider, or at least soft-pedal, these hot potatoes. He refused. "The voters have a right," he said, "to know where I stand on the issues." History, I feel certain, will record that his unswerving, implacable stand in his meetings with Gorbachev were key to the basic changes in Russia's policies.

Harriet and I were married in 1951, followed less than a year later by the Reagans. She and Nancy became close friends and it was during the next decade that the fabric of our friendship was built.

Evenings at the Reagans' house in the Pacific Palisades were invariably pleasant. People loved to go there. Ronnie often barbecued. He served excellent California wine, a custom he continued in the White House. There was always impromptu singing and entertainment. For some strange reason, years before anyone thought of Ronnie as a political figure Jack Benny referred to him as Governor. I never regarded Jack as a political pundit, but in this case he certainly read the tea leaves perfectly.

They, in turn, were a fixture when we entertained. When we moved to a new home in 1963 they were the first people, except for our houseguests Lee and Walter Annenberg, to sign our new guest book. He wrote, "We have no hesitation and indeed it is with pride that we take second billing to Lee and Walter and besides, we'd sign anything anywhere just to be at the Deutsches'. Ronald Reagan," to which Nancy added, "Me too." They subsequently signed the book very regularly indeed, but naturally had no premonition that it would become a marvelous bit of memorabilia.

Eggnogs on Christmas mornings at the Reagans' became a happy custom. It was there that we first met Nancy's parents, Edith and Loyal Davis, who annually came from Chicago for a holiday visit. They were a remarkable pair, almost disparate enough to classify as the "Odd Couple." Edith was a salty, feisty lady who had enjoyed a long acting career and retained many show-business friends. Loyal was a distinguished doctor who served as chief of staff at Chicago's Passavant Hospital. From her mother Nancy inherited a push toward her career, although it never really took firm root. Her father gave her an overall view of life that has stood her in good stead.

She took great pride in Loyal's career, the honors he achieved and, above all, his qualities as a father. Her grief at his death in 1982 was consuming, compounded by the fact that she was fairly certain she had cancer but could not confide in him at that stage of his life.

The attempted assassination of the President was without question the most traumatic event of Nancy's years in Washington. However, Edith Davis' death in 1987 was absolutely devastating. Edith was frail, her passing far from unexpected, but their relationship was an extremely close one. The timing, which can never be good, came right on the heels of Nancy's mastectomy. She flew from Washington to Phoenix in a state of shock at a time when most women who have undergone this surgery are in the midst of recuperating. None of us who flew to Phoenix will forget the vulnerable, grief-stricken face we saw at the church and at the Davis home later.

A minor happening that tickles the ribs enough to stick to them is part of the fabric of friendship. One beautiful summer evening in the late 1950s we drove with the Reagans to their Lake Malibu ranch. Ronnie's agent of many years and his wife drove up separately and joined us. After a wonderful barbecue supper we sat in the quiet of the screened-in porch. The only sound to be heard was the agent's audible breathing, a result I assume of emphysema.

Harriet, who is sometimes given to these inopportune utterances, said, "Isn't this peaceful and lovely? Just listen to the crickets." The rest of us, of course, knew where the noise was coming from. The agent, however, after listening intently, said, "I don't hear any crickets," to which Harriet responded, "I can't believe it. They're louder than ever." Soon afterward, the evening over, we left the ranch for the drive back to Los Angeles. We hadn't gone forty yards before Ronnie, who was driving, had to pull the car over to the side of the road, where the three of us collapsed laughing. Harriet at first thought we had gone mad. Then, on hearing the truth about the cricket noises, she was undone. For a long time any mention of the "cricket evening" did not amuse her at all.

Shortly after Ronnie's marriage his career hit the skids. It is an occupational hazard, but in his case it was partly propelled by the fact that he was extremely active as President of the Screen Actors Guild. Later he could truthfully say that he was the only candidate for President of the United States who had been president of a union, but he paid a steep price to make that point. Warner Bros. and other studios began to regard him more as a labor negotiator than a leading man.

During this fallow period he appeared in Las Vegas for several years quite successfully, but he always felt like a fish out of water. He also broadcast the Rose Bowl Parade from Pasadena extremely early on New Year's morning with, of all people, Bess Myerson. Nancy regularly invited us to see the New Year in with them at their Huntington Hotel suite, join Ronnie the next morning for the last part of the parade, and go on to the game. Since she was always a prime target for teasing, I would outline in a totally exaggerated way our exciting plans, while explaining that this Pasadena caper was a mediocre invitation at best. Years later when I reminded her of it she looked at me quizzically and said, "In the light of everything that's happened, do you still think it was such a dreadful invitation?" I had no choice but to tell her that, with hindsight, I had underrated it by a wide margin.

Ronnie's career took a formidable upward turn when he became the host of the General Electric Theatre in 1954. Television in those days was quite a comedown from films, but Ronnie, with typical Reagan luck, had no choice but to do it. The show was a big hit and GE expanded his role to speaking at their plants and in other venues. He loved the job; it was a natural for him. Handsome, attractive and, as the whole world was to learn, a superb, charismatic speaker, he became a successful rookie on the mashed-potato circuit. A lifelong Democrat, he rethought his political views as he met the top GE brass and eventually switched his party affiliation.

In 1964 Ronnie made a speech for Barry Goldwater that changed forever the course of the Reagans' lives. Goldwater was beyond help, but the morning after that speech the drumbeat to move Ronnie from the private sector to the public sector got under way. It never let up. In fact, it grew constantly louder and more insistent. His backers at first found themselves dealing with a reluctant noncandidate filled with self-doubt and uncertain about such a drastic turn in his career. Finally, he and Nancy could hold out no longer. The famous kitchen cabinet was born. To this day I am asked if I was a member.

I was not; in fact, I was in a completely different kitchen. Like Ronnie, I had always been a registered Democrat and his conversion did not carry me with him. He moved inexorably to become the Republican nominee for governor, running against the incumbent Pat Brown in 1966.

It was an occasion for unbridled joy to all his friends except me, for whom it posed an immediate problem. I decided, against Harriet's strong advice, to meet the problem head-on. I invited the Reagans for dinner (Harriet refused to make the call), telling them I had something most important to discuss with them. We dined at our house. I had hoped to take the matter up over coffee, but before long they both began to query me as to what it was all about.

I told Ronnie that I could not vote for him, saying that he was too conservative for me and making it very clear that I would never vote for his opponent. I told them I realized that it would end our friendship since, if the situation were reversed, I would be deeply hurt. Ronnie immediately told me to vote for anybody I wanted to. Nothing, he said, would break our friendship. Nancy behaved much more normally. She did not like it one bit. Deeply hurt, she simply stared at me unbelievingly. Harriet burst into tears. It was not a joyous evening. Nancy, to her everlasting credit, never mentioned it, refusing to permit it to wreck our relationship. Ronnie was swept into office without the benefit of my vote and we were very much a part of the festive proceedings in Sacramento the night he was sworn in.

It was an exciting evening. Marion and Earle Jorgensen, staunch Reagan supporters and close friends, hosted a festive dinner at the Fire House, a wonderful local restaurant. Ronnie was sworn in at one minute past midnight "to stop Pat Brown from appointing any more judges." We adjourned to the Governor's mansion, which turned out to be a dilapidated, drafty building featuring a splendid view of a gas station and a traffic light, and the unceasing rumble of passing trucks. No one ever worked harder for the right to live in substandard housing, a problem that was improved over time.

At the time none of us realized that our friends were embarking on a twenty-year journey that would make Los Angeles a home port rather than a home. This was least noticeable during Ronnie's eight years as governor. Nancy commuted regularly and their house was used during holidays and vacation time. By this time, of course, I was firmly aboard the Reagan political bandwagon.

The demand for Ronnie to run for President in 1976 started immediately. By the final two years of his second term it was a crescendo. Both of them were torn by doubts; a return to the private sector was not without appeal. Finally, under great pressure, Ronnie agreed to challenge President Ford in 1976. The result, when boiled down, meant eight years of campaigning, losing the first time and winning hugely the second. For Nancy eight years of life on the road was a trial. She missed home, family, friends, and did not overcome her fear of public speaking for a long time.

Distance is no ally to the maintenance of close relationships. A great deal of effort is required to till the soil. Nancy was determined to maintain her California friendships. She saw her friends whenever possible. A world-class telephone devotee, she made calls and returned calls from hotels and motels across America, as well as from the White House. I cannot recall a Christmas, a birthday, or an anniversary that did not bring with it a Reagan gift.

On election night it was an excited group that gathered at the Jorgensens'. The plan was to watch the early returns with the Reagans over a buffet supper, then on by bus to the Century Plaza Hotel to sweat it out. Happily, this turned out to be unnecessary. By six-thirty P.M. all three networks had declared Ronnie a landslide winner. He walked in with Nancy to be cheered for the first time as the fortieth President of the United States. The VIP suite at the Century Plaza was not a sweatbox but a comfortable place to view the ballroom celebration.

January 20th, 1981, the day of Ronnie's first Inauguration, will always remain a high point of my life. There are in our United States several hundred million Americans. Since we have only one President at a time, the odds against knowing a First Family intimately over decades defy calculation. Nancy, coping with incredibly complex demands, made certain that every detail of the day was perfectly planned for her California friends.

At nine-thirty A.M. we entered the St. James Episcopal Church, known as the Presidents' Church, a beautiful, simple, small house of worship. There was room for only the Reagans, the Bushes, their families, the new official family, and the Reagan friends. The Reagans solemnly entered the church to take their places. Within a few hours Ronnie would assume the highest office in the land. He would no longer be Ronnie to me, but Mr. President. Nancy's name would remain the same, but she would be the First Lady.

After the service we were escorted by a lady Marine to a small bus, gaily festooned with red, white, and blue bunting, that would be our home for the day. We crawled through the pandemonium past endless check points to the Inaugural stands. Our seats were so close that we were virtually part of the proceedings. Gradually the distinguished guests began to take their places. Nancy was escorted down the Capitol steps to her seat. Vice President–elect Bush, his wife, and the Supreme Court Justices followed. There was a hushed expectant silence. For a moment Nancy's eyes swept over her California friends. Suddenly Ronnie appeared on the podium.

The transfer of power in America, blessedly simple, is the envy of much of the world. After Vice President Bush had been sworn in, Ronnie stepped forward. Chief Justice Warren F. Burger administered the oath as Nancy stood beside him. The *New York Times* reported that as the President began his inaugural address the sun burst through the January clouds that generally cover Washington. Soon it was over. The Marine band played "Hail to the Chief." There was hardly a dry eye in our group as the President turned and walked up the steps of the Capitol.

Back in the bus again, we were driven to a secluded spot on the White House grounds for box lunches and a glass of California white wine. The final stop of our day was the Presidential reviewing stand. It was packed, but we were seated down front, an extended branch of the Reagan family. The traditional parade was exciting and heartwarming. Finally the Reagans stood up. After warm goodbyes to all, they were gone. The three-thousand-mile move from San Onofre Drive in the Pacific Palisades to 1600 Pennsylvania Avenue in Washington was a fait accompli. Two close friends and neighbors had very definitely left town.

The second time around, the President won every state except Minnesota and the District of Columbia. The traditional Jorgensen buffet was low key and happy. No one minded the absence of drama one bit. Even with the bus ride to the Century Plaza Hotel, it was an early-to-bed evening.

The weatherman was the key player at the second Inauguration. It was so bitter cold that all outdoor events had to be canceled. The President was sworn in for his second term in the Capitol rotunda, which could accommodate but a fraction of the ticket holders. Harriet and I stood less than six feet from him as he took the oath of office. A fleeting thought passed through my mind. Whoever became President four years from that day would have no reserved place set aside for me. I would not be six feet from the President; twenty-five hundred miles was the more likely distance. This was the moment to drink it all in.

During the Reagan years I served as Vice Chairman of the President's Committee on the Arts and the Humanities. Nancy was our Honorary Chairman; the accent was definitely meant to be on the first word. Every committee of this sort, and there are thousands of them, yearns for a direct route over the head of the bureaucracy that often stands as a barrier to accomplishment. I had that access. I used it to the hilt, generally but not always stopping just short of abusing it.

A typical frustration stemmed from the fact that White House personnel always had a barrel of names of staunch Reagan supporters eager to be of service. Occasionally, with the best of intentions, they would fill a vacancy on our committee with someone who did not know the difference between a painting and a concert. When all else failed, I made an appointment to go to the White House to prevail on our Honorary Chairman to intervene by letting us have a voice in choosing new committee members. This was miles from her designated role, the kind of nuts-and-bolts item that should not involve her. It was an imposition, but friendship prevailed and she paved the way for me. We had able people on our committee.

Our initial White House invitation was to attend a small reception the day following the first Inauguration. It was an exciting experience. During the next eight years Nancy saw to it that many such invitations came our way. Harriet and I attended state dinners, luncheons, receptions, and musical performances. We watched the 4th of July fireworks from the Truman Balcony. We quite often visited the First Family's living quarters which, among other things, provide an intimate glimpse of American history. Together with the Walter Annenbergs, Earle Jorgensens, and William Wilsons, we hosted the President's seventieth and seventy-fifth birthday parties at the White House. I cannot imagine anyone becoming blasé about visiting the White House. I know it always made my heart beat faster.

Four years to the day after the second Inauguration "the Reagan friends" joined a large group of invited guests to see them fly in on Air Force One for their return to Southern California and private life. The following Saturday night at a small dinner party the President said he had a brief story for us.

"When I went to my first Economic Summit shortly after going to Washington I noticed that everyone was on a first-name basis. It was 'Margaret, Helmut, François, Brian, etc.' Everyone but me. I was the new kid on the block. They all called me 'Mr. President.' Finally, I had the opportunity to say to them, 'Look, ladies and gentlemen, my name is Ron. And I'm saying exactly that to all of you now.' "

Is everything the same? Not quite. World leaders come by to call. No matter the degree of informality, everyone gets up when Ronnie enters the room. On the golf course members of his foursome, for some reason, drift back to "Mr. President." He tees off first even if he got an eleven on the preceding hole.

Nancy's schedule is extremely varied and, I feel, far too busy for her own good. I complain to her, as do her other friends, that she does not eat enough. This is a far cry indeed from the girl who rolled up a five-dollar check in the MGM commissary in 1949. My friend has been on quite a journey since we lunched together that day.

# ME
*and*
# BOGART

ALMOST FROM THE time I arrived in Hollywood from New York I was accepted into large segments of the film industry elite. This, though I only fully realized it later on, was no mean feat. For many reasons, most of them valid, these luminaries were with rare exceptions at ease only with one another. Theirs was a closed society second only to Gorky before Gorbachev. The fact that I knew quite a few of the membership from their New York trips was certainly a factor in my slipping through the silk curtain. Whatever the reasons, it was an extremely pleasant facet of my newly transplanted life since they entertained constantly.

If I had expected to find wild Hollywood parties, which I did not, I would have been badly off target. These gatherings were, if possible, more decorous than those I had left behind. The flower arrangements were lavish and the menus excellent. There was endless shop talk, but really no more than a group of Wall Streeters or lawyers produced.

The singular difference was the glowing and beautiful appearance of the guests. Take a random sampling from a mix of Clark Gable, David Niven, Loretta Young, Robert Taylor, Barbara Stanwyck, Fred Astaire, Cary Grant, Deborah Kerr, Gary Cooper, and the Bogarts and one does not come up short in the looks department. This was toned down a bit by the presence of leading producers and directors who simply looked like other normal people. Writers were never invited.

Among these dazzling equals, Lauren Bacall and Humphrey Bogart always seemed a touch more equal than the others. They were sought after to the point where they represented a security blanket to hostesses. If the Bogarts were present, the evening seemed destined for success.

They were very different from one another and yet they complemented each other perfectly. Betty brought to the party her tawny beauty, husky voice, ready laugh, and ribald humor. She also brought her husband. Bogart was Bogart, which was more than enough.

There is in Jean Howard's splendid book *Hollywood, a Photo Memoir* one picture that says it all. Betty, looking like a young tigress, is lying on the grass at a Sunday luncheon, Bogie seated behind her. The other "Sunday stars" (Ms. Howard's words) are grouped around them for all the world like a supporting cast. The Bogarts were stars to the stars.

Betty made some major changes, and all for the better, in the irascible, hard-drinking Bogie. His previous marriage to actress Mayo Methot had been distinguished by epic fights that often drew spectacular press coverage. Although she tamed him quite a bit, he was, to put it mildly, never a threat to the charming, debonair politeness of David Niven.

All went well with my busy social schedule for quite a while. I was, of course, aware that I had a producer's job at MGM through pull, in sharp contrast to the rest of the group, who made their fame and fortune the old-fashioned way. They earned it. I simply assumed that this was understood and unspoken, which, with Bogart present, was like believing in the tooth fairy. "Listen, kid," he said to me one evening, "don't confuse inheriting money with having talent." His tone was pleasant, but that smile which chilled audiences throughout the world was not something he left at the studio. The other guests were used to Bogart's brutal needling, but I was shocked and mortified. A few discreet inquiries disclosed the fact that Bogart never insulted underlings but often went for the jugular with his peers. The problem was that I had no feeling of being his peer. On the contrary. My dominant emotion was an enormous and totally justified insecurity, which I was able to contain until confronted.

Bogart had an uncanny ability to smell blood when his attacks were damaging his victim. On those occasions he became a veritable pit bull. He never lost an opportunity to further enlighten me on the difference between inherited wealth and talent. My feelings gradually changed from embarrassment to anger. Inevitably the evening came when I had had enough. "Listen, Bogie," I said in the time-honored language of such confrontations, "I've had it with you. Don't talk to me again. Not ever. Not about anything." Kirk Douglas remembers to this day that as I started toward him he grabbed a pair of glasses from the man next to him. Putting them on, he said to me, "It's not right to hit an older man." Others quickly intervened. Bogart could not have been happier. He had scored a bull's-eye with relative ease. My wrath maintained itself at a remarkably high level. I pictured him knocked out by me and lying on a terrace battered, bleeding, and repentant. It was, of course, a scene not destined for fulfillment.

Inevitably I saw him a few nights later. He was sitting on a sofa with a few other men. Those Hollywood dinner parties were like Quaker meetings. The men bonded together and the women did the same. "Good evening," he greeted me politely. "How are you?" This was my moment. "I told you never to speak to me again," and I went for him. Of course, I never got close to him. Cooler heads stood between us and I had to content myself with a stream of invective. Bogart remained quietly on the couch, but he had the last word. "You should never strike a smaller man," he said. "It's a cowardly thing to do."

Within a very few days my "affaire Bogart" took a dramatic and fatal turn. Word spread like wildfire that he had been stricken by incurable cancer. I felt shocked and genuinely sorry for him, but I was selfish enough to feel rather sorry for myself. What had I ever done to deserve being caught in a quarrel of that nature with a man who instantly became terminally ill? It was extremely hard to remember that I was the wronged party when the life of my adversary was drawing to a close.

Bogart had a large coterie of friends who cared for him very much indeed and called on him regularly. Word spread of his gallantry and unfailing good humor. One night, for example, I heard John Huston, his closest friend, say proudly that he had never seen the like of it. I should, of course, have written him and indeed tried many times. None of my efforts seemed just right, so I never mailed a letter, and in time one could say I learned to live with Bogart's illness.

Hollywood in those days was still a fight town and sometimes attracted prestigious events. A middleweight championship fight was scheduled at this time, and Frank Sinatra seized upon it to host a fight party. The guests were to meet at Romanoff's restaurant for drinks and hors d'oeuvres and then go off in limos to the fight. At Romanoff's people were saying that Bogart would make an appearance. It seemed implausible to me and I hoped it was just a rumor. Not so. Suddenly a large, pillowed chair appeared and very shortly Bogart was helped in and sat down. It was an awesome moment. This world-famous actor, haggard and emaciated, looked around the room, his eyes bright and defiant. Without plan, we formed a ragged line so that each of us could speak with him briefly. I dreaded my turn, but inevitably and very quickly I found myself standing in front of him. He spoke immediately. "Don't worry about it, kid. Those things happen. It was just bad timing for you, for both of us as a matter of fact." I stood there flabbergasted and tried without success to speak. "It's okay, kid," he said. "Forget it." I moved on but he called me back, eyes twinkling. "Remember, kid, it's better to inherit money than to have talent." He could not let it be. It was too much for me, coming from this man so close to his death. I went swiftly to the men's room and cried. I never saw him again. I never knew him well, hardly at all really. I wish I had.

Casablanca is my favorite movie. I run it often and every single time I relive that evening. I remember him well.

# ME

*and*

# BENNETT CERF

In 1967 Harriet and I took a trip to the Far East with Phyllis and Bennett Cerf. Bennett was at this juncture a full-fledged celebrity, a status he dearly loved. One day in Kyoto our guide took us to see a holy shrine, surrounded by the usual busloads of people. We were proceeding toward the entrance when we lost Bennett. I found him completely surrounded by a group of Americans, all eagerly seeking his autograph. I told him we were eager to move along. He told us to go ahead. "I like what I'm doing," he said. No statement could ever define more accurately the prism through which he saw life.

Happiness is an elusive goal. We are all in a Mixmaster of highs and lows, ups and downs, boredom and excitement, with the negatives predominating. No one bothered to explain this to Bennett Cerf, and he lived his life without ever finding it out. He is the only human being I ever met who took it for granted that he would have a wonderful time from the moment he woke up in the morning until he fell asleep, which was the moment his head hit the pillow. Except for occasional visits to the dentist, life very rarely let him down.

The Random House Dictionary defines envy as "a desire for some advantage possessed by another." We were extremely close friends for over forty years, yet I constantly envied his seamless life of pleasure, at the heart of which was hard work in a field he loved. The simplicity with which the compartments of his life melded defies analysis. There was no complicated, labored machinery and no sand in the gears. To describe his disposition as sunny comes no closer to the heart of the matter than saying that Einstein was not stupid. Simply put, Bennett was blessed, and it is best to leave it at that.

His parents, pleasantly well-to-do New Yorkers, doted on

him. After high school graduation, Bennett was already far too devout a New Yorker to leave town for a college education. He enrolled at Columbia, choosing the School of Journalism because they did not require geometry. Any institution that made math a required subject would have denied him further education.

His march through college was a harbinger of what lay ahead for this man for all seasons. He was quickly elected to his fraternity of choice, chosen vice president of his sophomore class, and made Phi Beta Kappa his junior year. Of far greater importance, he became editor of the school newspaper, for which he wrote a column and started a book review section.

To please his father, he made a brief false start in Wall Street. After a very short time he convinced his father that he was totally miscast and got a job with a publisher, Horace Liveright. Never destined to be a serious lasting figure, Liveright pointed the way to the eager young neophyte. It was probably Liveright's greatest achievement as a publisher. Unfortunately, his approach to his work was in many ways that of a dilettante. Bennett learned early on that, while publishing sounded glamorous, it took hard daily application to stay afloat.

Liveright was an attractive, popular man. It was through him that Bennett originally met the first of the exciting people who were to populate his life. The slightest opening of the door was all he needed. He was drawn into waiting arms and was soon accepted into the world that was to be his oyster. Shortly afterward came the opportunity to buy the Modern Library, precursor to Random House. He and a partner purchased it at an excellent price and Bennett, despite his God-given light touch, started a lifelong regimen of hard work.

The name Random House accurately reflected his plan. As he noted in his posthumously published memoir, *At Random*, he would publish random books he enjoyed, hoping that other readers would share his taste. His judgment was validated often enough to build Random House into a front-rank, multi-million-dollar publishing giant.

At the core of everything that made up his character was his ongoing love affair with books. Reading was an unmitigated pleasure to him. Leonora Hornblow, one of his dearest friends, collaborated with him on two excellent anthologies. One day they were hard at work when Bennett looked at her and, smiling happily, said, "Aren't we lucky? We get to read these great stories, talk about them and then read them again." He admired good writing. He revered great writing. He took unending joy in giving new talent a chance. He cared deeply about a book's presentation; the cover, the jacket, the type of print, the quality of paper, the advertising, promotion, distribution, and selling of books all fascinated him.

Will Rogers said, "I never met a man I didn't like." Bennett rarely met a writer he didn't like. The core of his publishing talent was his ability to relate to writers. He once said, "Close to sixty or eighty percent of the time with any novelist or playwright is devoted to talking about the author's work. Obviously a writer loves to talk about himself and it's a publisher's business to let him. That was the life I had chosen for myself and when authors were talking about themselves and their books or plays I was in heaven, so we got along very well."

The Random House list of authors over the decades is far too long to enumerate, but such diverse individuals as William Faulkner, Robinson Jeffers, James Joyce, Sinclair Lewis, Ayn Rand, John O'Hara, James Michener, Gertrude Stein, and Truman Capote all found a sensitive, caring, knowledgeable friend in their publisher.

That is not to say that it was all ham and jam. William Faulkner, for example, was famous for his bouts with the bottle. When no one could deal with him, or even find him, Bennett would venture into Faulkner country, the deep South, sober him up, straighten him out, and travel north until the next time. This was not a great trial for Bennett. With his God-given gift for oversimplification, he simply regarded it as part of the work of being Faulkner's publisher.

Sinclair Lewis, cantankerous and also a drunkard, came to Random House from Doubleday, where he had written some truly great books. He had won the Nobel Prize for Literature in 1930 with such entries as *Main Street*, *Arrowsmith*, *Elmer Gantry*, and *Dodsworth*. Bennett's chest puffed out when he was able to put him on the Random House list of authors. For a long time Lewis combined fallow periods with mediocre books. He finally produced two perfectly marvelous novels, *Cass Timberlane* and *Kingsblood Royal*, which together did not nearly make up for the long nonproductive periods. Bennett never gave up on him; where truly superior writers were involved he refused to judge everything by the bottom line. Part of Bennett's productivity lay in the fact that he despised and refused to attend large meetings. He preferred small get-togethers in his office. These usually involved differences of opinion. Since Bennett did not regard these as problems, he almost always came up with a suggestion that got everyone back on the right track.

Editors are an essential cog in the publishing process. They can be, Bennett attested, almost as temperamental as their writers, but these interrelationships run deep. Random House had their complement of splendid editors. Perhaps the most famous is Jason Epstein. When Epstein was at Doubleday, Bennett got word that he was unhappy. He called the Doubleday publisher, who warned him saying, "He's a wonderful boy, but he will drive you crazy. He's almost driven me crazy." Bennett could not put Epstein out of his mind, knowing that he was a superb piece of manpower indigenous to the literary elite of the city. Shortly after he recruited Epstein he learned that the Doubleday publisher was right on target. This pleased Bennett rather than irritating him. He referred to Epstein as "the cross I bear." Epstein retaliated by referring to Bennett as "the bear I cross." Bennett summed it all up airily by saying that Jason "does things his own way and anyone who tries to stop him is wasting his breath." Having him at Random House did not drive Bennett crazy at all; he enjoyed it very much.

In 1940 Bennett married Phyllis Fraser in what proved to be his shining moment. Phyllis, a cousin of Ginger Rogers and raised with her, had a very brief career as a Hollywood starlet. She disliked the life, moved to New York, and when Bennett met her she had started to write and was working on two popular daytime radio serials.

Bennett was smitten immediately, but he was a gun-shy suitor. A few years earlier he had made one of his few missteps, marrying screen star Sylvia Sidney. It was doomed to failure from the start. It was less than a year before Bennett realized that he was never meant to be the husband of a movie star and they went their separate ways. Still, it left scars.

Bennett could not help but notice that his friends, and the number of them stunned Phyllis, adored her. He took considerable ribbing throughout this period because Phyllis was fifteen years his junior, and looked far younger than that. The inevitable marriage vows were administered by New York City Mayor Fiorello La Guardia at City Hall.

Blessed with a high energy level, she was from the start able to cope with her hugely busy, gregarious husband, the household, and the two fine sons who came along. She became an integral part of Random House, making her mark primarily as an editor in the field of children's books, particularly the famous Dr. Seuss.

Although it was furthest from his mind, Bennett struck a mighty blow for me when he married Phyllis. Over the decades our friendship has been meaningful and dear to me. We try to telephone each week. Whenever Harriet and I let her know that we are coming to New York, her response is immediate. "We'll have a marvelous party for you. Save the first day for lunch. Let me look at my book to see what we're doing and what you might enjoy." If my life depended on it, I could not remember where I first met Bennett and Phyllis. It seems to me I have known them always.

Extolling her virtues as a friend would be an elaborate process. It is perhaps better to speak of a grievous flaw in my dear friend. She is a dreadful, gloating winner in backgammon, and an even worse loser. She is a rotten sport, but I am little better.

Bennett did not rest on his publishing laurels. Early on he started a newspaper column that was widely syndicated. He became a prodigious writer. Humor was always near and dear to his heart. A sampling of his titles speak for themselves: *Laugh Day, Out on a Limerick, The Laugh's on Me, Good for a Laugh, Laughter Incorporated,* and *Laughingstock.*

Random House could not, of course, publish his books. Doubleday and Harper & Row usually filled that function. Sitting on the author's side of the desk, he peppered his own publishers with the same complaints he constantly faced from

222 ★ ARMAND DEUTSCH

Random House authors. "Why," he would ask, "isn't my book better advertised and better promoted? Why was the first printing so small? Why don't I ever see it in the window of a bookstore?" This role reversal was so total that neither author Cerf nor his publishers could get through a single session without laughing. They invariably wound up talking about mutual publishing problems.

The icing on Bennett's already delicious cake came in 1950 with the advent of *What's My Line?* The pioneer TV game show producer Mark Goodson took a chance on Bennett, as he did indeed on all his panelists, and Bennett did not let him down. He was a hit from the start. "Audiences," Goodson fondly reminisces, "saw in him just what I saw, an urbane, sophisticated, humorous man with the common touch. They welcomed him into their homes. Bennett and I had an even trade-off. He introduced me to New Yorkers I would never have met and I introduced him to the American public." As Bennett became a fixture in millions of homes, his recognition factor leaped from that of an unknown to a very real celebrity. He loved it with a typical, unabashed joy. Walking into a theatre, he would exclaim unbelievingly, "They know me! They know me!" It did not change him one iota. It did add immeasurably to an already pleasant, exciting life.

From the start Bennett was a dreadful, unremitting punster. His friends would groan when he began one, but they could not resist smiling at his joy and infectious laughter even if they winced at the end.

During his years on *What's My Line?* his punning brought the same reaction from national television audiences. Lo and behold, the result was a book titled *Bennett Cerf's Treasury of Atrocious Puns.* It sold extremely well and the publishers, Messrs. Harper & Row, explained the reason in their foreword: "To countless Americans who suffer from the same affliction of punning, Bennett Cerf is a friend indeed. They can evade a small measure of culpability for every horrendous pun they spawn by winding it up with a resigned comment that even Bennett Cerf wouldn't stoop that low." They urged their readers not to read too many puns at one sitting since there is a limit to every man's endurance.

A random sampling suffices to explain the sales phenomenon:

Bulldozing: Falling asleep during a political speech.

Camelot: A place where they park camels.

Exchequer: A retired supermarket employee.

I would like to reaffirm my belief in Buddha. But, on the other hand, there is a great deal to be said for margarine.

An eccentric bachelor passed away and left his nephew nothing but 392 clocks. The nephew is now busy winding up the estate.

A high school drop-out landed a job that takes a lot of guts. He puts strings on electric guitars.

"There's one thing about taking dictation from my boss," sighed a secretary. "You have to take a lot for grunted."

"Know why the prettiest nurse at St. Luke's Hospital is known as 'Appendix'? Only the doctors are allowed to take her out."

A stone quarry owner was arrested for overcharging. He was taking too much for granite.

Before long he was in great demand on the lecture circuit. Most people on the tour regard it as an inconvenient way to make money or to promote something. Not so with Bennett. He lapped it up. The travel, the lectures, and the adulation were meat and drink to him. He prepared three or four excellent lectures and gave each of them two titles, enabling his lecture bureau to send out an impressive list. He kept meticulous files so that he was never in danger of returning to a city for the second time and giving the same lecture under a different title.

The popular term "networking" did not exist during this period, but no one was ever better at it than Bennett. He never visited a city without going the next day to as many bookshops as possible. The huge chains and discount booksellers had not yet taken over. Most of the shops were independent and often run by what Bennett referred to as "little old ladies in tennis shoes." Bennett often complained about the primitive way that books were distributed, but he turned it to his advantage. When he appeared unannounced everyone was thrilled to see him. They shared a great common bond. Unlike their modern-day counterparts, who are cashiers and might as well be selling oranges, they, like Bennett, read the books.

Anyone old enough and lucky enough to have dealt with a saleslady who read the books was spoiled forever. My friendship with Mrs. Brandt at Martindale's bookshop in Beverly Hills was more meaningful to me than I ever realized at the time. She knew my tastes and set books aside for me. When I went in we chatted about books. She was the copilot of my reading habits. Mrs. Brandt is long gone; the Martindale site is now a glitzy women's boutique. I still buy books, but the fun has gone out of it. I miss it.

Bennett enjoyed chatting with bookshop people, always pleading that Random House books receive better shelf space and more sales effort. His departure from the shop did not mean that he passed from their lives. He maintained careful files, writing, phoning, and forming them into his own network. No publisher before, during, or since ever knew as many retailers as he did.

From the television program came the lectures. From the lectures came the bookshop tours. From the bookshop tours came increased sales of Random House books. Synergy, thy name is Cerf.

Bennett unabashedly collected people who enhanced his life. As a rule of thumb, people who try to chart this course are forced to go about it in a clumsy, obvious manner that is a prescription for failure. Not so with Bennett. It came as naturally to him as breathing. He saw no advantage in being with boring people and, since he himself was a world-class life-enhancer, it all melded perfectly.

The Cerfs for decades had a warm, welcoming salon. With the host and hostess setting the tone, parties at their home were a mecca with the best and brightest creative people in the city.

Truman Capote's social celebrity was born on one of these evenings. Many men canceled, all with valid reasons, but Phyl-

lis was determined not to give a "ladies'" dinner. She called
Bennett and ordered him to round up a few Random House
writers.

At cocktails the butler told Phyllis that there was a child at
the door. "That," proclaimed Bennett, "is Truman." Capote's
novel *Other Voices, Other Rooms* had just appeared to outstanding reviews. The "child," with his high-pitched voice and
Southern accent, took over the party. All present were mes-
merized and Truman's emergence as a literary lion began. Bennett accurately said that "Truman never dined alone again."

Conversation always flourished. So did superb entertainment that usually got under way as performers drifted in from
their shows. No one questioned that Bennett's favorite people
on earth were writers. No one but me. I always felt that the
people he most cherished were the songwriters. These evenings
peaked for him when one of them took over. He just beamed.
When Richard Rodgers played some of his extraordinary
songs, Bennett invariably said, "I can't believe this. Dick
Rodgers playing the piano in my house." The two were good
friends since college days and Rodgers was a staple at these
evenings. There was nothing feigned, however, about Bennett's reaction. As his son Jonathan said, "He would have been
a very poor liar. His face was always a perfect mirror of his
thoughts. What you saw was what you got."

Immodestly I have to admit that I must have been one of
the people who Bennett felt enhanced his life. He certainly
enhanced mine, as did Phyllis. I can safely claim the title of
being the most frequent houseguest at that wonderful home
on East 62nd Street. Almost every time I went to New York
without Harriet I stayed there. It is easy to get lonely in a hotel.
This was a household that embraced its guests, and as Bennett
often courteously told me, the price was right. A single memory seems to summarize countless others.

I came downstairs for breakfast to find Bennett reading the
*New York Times*. I sat down, we grunted hello, I ordered my
breakfast and picked up my copy of the paper. Neither of us
looked up until I noticed a toast rack in front of me. I was
chewing away contentedly when Bennett looked up and said
irately, "Why, you son of a bitch, you've eaten my breakfast."

I told Bennett that this was no way to talk to or treat a beloved houseguest.

That evening we went to the Tony Randalls' for dinner. I told everyone how ill-treated I was at the Cerfs' and could not even get bread for breakfast. The next day Randall sent me a huge deluxe package of food delicacies with a note saying that he hoped it would hold me over the hard times. I showed it to Bennett with great satisfaction, asking that it be put in my room. Bennett countermanded by instructions by having the entire thing unpacked and put in the kitchen. "You're eating us out of house and home," he said. The next day he dashed off a note to Randall denouncing him as being gullible and informing him that the wrong person had received the care package. That cannot happen to a guest in a hotel.

In 1965 the four of us took a trip to Brazil. We traveled happily together but were not immune to misadventures. Bennett was invariably our travel agent. On this particular trip, however, I informed him that Jorge Guinle, the owner of Rio's Copacabana Hotel, the only deluxe hotel at that time, was a friend of mine. He dismissed this airily. "You are dealing with a huge television star. Leave everything in my hands."

The flight was, and remains, the longest of my life. Planes were slower then and we waited seven hours in a blinding New York snowstorm before taking off. We landed, tired and grumpy, in the heat and blinding sunshine of the Brazilian summer. Our first tiny premonition that all was not in hand came when the hotel limousines, promised us by travel agent Cerf, did not meet us. We loaded our luggage and ourselves into two rickety taxicabs for the long drive, which took us past the filthy squalor of Rio's *favelas* and finally onto the road fronting that world-famous beach and to the entrance of the hotel.

Bennett, unshaven and seedy-looking in his rumpled New York suit, made his way to the reservation desk. The handsome clerks in gleaming white uniforms made us feel like Ellis Island immigrants. Bennett authoritatively announced our names. An interminably long check of the reservation books did not reveal the name of either Cerf or Deutsch. It was the height of the season and the hotel was booked for weeks ahead. Bennett fought like a tiger, but in what seemed the twinkling of an eye, we passed out of the cool, grand lobby and back into the taxicabs. Ten minutes later we were deposited at a hotel recommended as "not excellent," but "good." "Good," it turned out, meant dirty rooms, dingy walls, sleazy bathrooms, and beds that dared one to lie down. We sat gingerly on the room's grimy two chairs, listening through the paper-thin walls as Phyllis, ably representing the three of us, laced into Bennett.

Harriet broke the silence. "We have got to bribe those swanky-looking men," she said firmly. I praised her as though she had discovered the Rosetta Stone. While taxiing back to the Copacabana we debated on what would be considered a lavish amount. We decided that one hundred American dollars should do the trick. In Brazilian currency at that time we reasoned that they could buy a home in the country. Harriet, uncharacteristically, insisted on handling the transaction. I watched her buttering them up and cleverly flashing the cash. A very brief re-examination of the reservation book revealed that, blessedly, there had just been a cancellation. A beautiful two-bedroom suite was available. Harriet went to claim it instantly while I returned to the low-rent district to collect our baggage and inform the Cerfs of our upward mobility. Bennett asked me how we accomplished this feat. I said, "We gave him one hundred dollars. That's how we did it. Anyway, what difference does it make? Get your gear together. We're only ten minutes away from a shower."

Bennett very grandly said, "I'll pay for half of that." Bennett was simply quoting the rule that we always used when we traveled, so his offer to do what he had to do in any event angered me. I said, "Goddamn it, Bennett, you're going to pay for the whole thing. You screwed this up. We straightened it out and I want to be reimbursed for the entire amount." "Not on your life," said Bennett. "I'd rather stay here as a matter of principle than give in to that kind of blackmail." By the time he had finished the sentence Phyllis and I had pushed him out of the room.

Our suite was superb. It seemed far better to us than if we had gotten it the first time around. The trip was all we had hoped for. Bennett stood firm and paid for only half the bribe.

On another of our trips, this time to the Orient, Bennett was, as usual, in charge of our reservations. He invariably requested a two-bedroom suite. The first time one bedroom was inferior we would flip a coin. The loser got the poorer room. From then on we alternated, keeping meticulous records.

We arrived in Hong Kong late one afternoon after a long flight and went directly to the newly built, luxurious Mandarin Hotel, where our master logistic expert had booked the top-of-the-line Mandarin Suite. The living room was enormous, beautifully furnished, and offered a postcard view of the bay with its endless traffic from sampans to ocean liners. I had a sneaking feeling that this particular accommodation was used mostly for corporate receptions and cocktail parties. It had been duly recorded that it was our turn for the better room, and better it was. A huge bedroom overlooking the bay, an outsized black marble bathroom and closet space for a month's stay. It was virtually a suite in itself.

Rather timorously we set out on the long trek across the living room in search of the Cerf bedroom. Regrettably, we found it. It was little more than a cubbyhole, obviously a servant's room for the rich folks at the other end. It was a jarring note, an accommodation inequity beyond our wildest dreams. Phyllis' reaction was tight-lipped but stoical. Bennett, that constant maker of bad jokes and puns, the enhancer of the lives of everyone around him with his smiling, laughing manner, could on occasion pout, frown, and be bad-tempered. These seldom-seen traits all came to the fore. I suggested that common sense dictated that they get a large double room across the hall. Bennett, tired from our journey, stubbornly refused, angrily pronouncing that the fun of the trip was being together.

Harriet and I quickly solved the problem by insisting that halfway through our six-day stay we switch. Bennett smiled, Phyllis was relieved, and we went back to our high-rent district to unpack. The moment we were alone I assured Harriet that I would book a room to be available to us on moving day.

We were collapsing with laughter when there came a sharp, rather hostile, knock on the door. It was Bennett. He sullenly inquired if we had any pressing or laundry to go out. We were puzzled. He explained that there had been a ring on his door. A smallish gentlemen had been sent by the management to learn Harriet's and my wishes. It sunk in on us that for the next three days all hotel help, including room service, could approach us only through ringing the doorbell of our newly acquired servants. Bennett stood in his silk robe at our door, his face suddenly taking on the aspect of an inquiring beagle hound. We laughed. We couldn't help it and Bennett, God bless him, joined in.

On our first evening in Hong Kong we were guests of the movie impresario Run Run Shaw. He politely urged us to check out of our hotel and be his houseguests. Bennett, to our stunned surprise, grandly replied that we couldn't. We had, he said, our heart's desire, the Mandarin Suite at the Mandarin Hotel. Phyllis' scathing look made us fear for his safety. Mr. Shaw dropped us off at our street of dreams and it was a rather subdued group that said their goodnights.

It was part of our routine that before we turned out our light, Bennett would knock on the door, enter, and deliver a heartfelt version of his favorite song of the moment, "You Are My Lucky Star." There was no lucky star that night.

Awakening ahead of Harriet the next morning, I quietly made my way into the vastness of our living room. Bennett was having breakfast in the middle of the room, trying unsuccessfully to contain a mounting anger. Off on one side a man was quietly going about the business of sweeping and brushing. I was determined to let the Random House publisher break the silence. Finally he did. "Tell that man," he exploded, "that you are not my master." Before getting into noisier work the man had inquired of Bennett if his master was up yet. Turning grandly, I told the "sweeper," as he became known to us, to proceed and then told Bennett to order my breakfast.

Worse was yet to come. On the evening of the second day, Harriet became ill. Not under the weather. Ill, really ill. Doctors were summoned by Run Run Shaw. Hospitalization was seriously considered. Finally, medication and total bed rest was deemed the proper course of action, together with prayers that Harriet could make the long Hong Kong/Los Angeles flight on schedule. She saw no more of Hong Kong. She did make the plane. We obviously did not move. The Cerfs remained in their humble quarters until the end.

We had planned a large and glamorous Hollywood tent party in their honor as they beat their way back to New York. They stayed with us in Los Angeles and again, although their room this time was fine, ours was better. As we walked in to dinner the night of the party, the orchestra played "You Are My Lucky Star." Bennett loved it.

Through the years the "sweeper" story was told with relish by both of us. Bennett sometimes hinted that Harriet's illness was trumped up. I asked just as often why he hadn't used better judgment and gotten another room. Invariably he responded that "the fun was being together."

Bennett died very suddenly in August 1971. He had been in the hospital only very briefly once before in his life. The *Saturday Review* said of him: "He set out to be a book publisher. He became one of the best. He gave full measure to his profession. Everyone connected with the world of books is in his debt." All of his close friends are perhaps even more deeply in his debt.

I have never quite been able to believe that Bennett, not yet thirty, founded Random House when I was only twelve years old. I have never met a younger man.

# ME
*and*
# MY ONE-NIGHTERS WITH SINATRA

My WIFE, HARRIET, and I enter New York's Waldorf Towers lobby at precisely 6:55 P.M. We are off on another one-nighter with Frank Sinatra.

We greet Frank, Barbara, his retinue, and the other guests who make up our party of twelve. A moment later we are in limousines, airport-bound. A Sinatra one-nighter is timed with the precision of a West Point dress parade. Logistics fascinate him. He would have made a superb travel agent, except that he never could have learned the importance of the cost factor in the travel plans of clients. His preoccupation is to get from here to there and back as quickly as possible.

This specific junket happened to be to Buffalo in 1977. I had long ago learned that the destination is basically immaterial. The one-nighters are as alike as peas in a pod. You land in the dark and you leave in the dark. Unless one knows the name of the city, the locales are totally interchangeable.

A few minutes after takeoff Frank is immersed in his cross-word puzzle, which he does rapidly and in ink. As always, he wears slacks, a pullover shirt, a windbreaker or sweater topped with a baseball or golf cap. His headgear collection—gifts from Major League teams, golf clubs, and tournaments—is inex-haustible, but he augments it by buying caps wherever he sees them. It is not that he is partial to caps—he stops just short of being a compulsive buyer. His purchases for himself are, how-ever, overmatched by those he makes for his friends.

As the plane speeds through the night, Harriet and I reflect on the treasure trove in our own home: several clocks affec-tionately inscribed and signed "Francis Albert," picture frames, a hi-fi system, a windbreaker bearing the slogan "American Olympic Drinking Team," countless tapes and recordings, and draft-beer system together with monthly supplies of the product.

One example of his generosity stands out. Some twenty-five years ago he was having a quiet dinner at our house when our son Stephen, then eleven, told me that he desperately required new sound equipment in his room. It was rather costly and I told him that we might consider it for Christmas. Sinatra said nothing, but the equipment arrived the next day, together with a note from Frank saying that a man would be over to connect it.

The next time we met, I told Frank that I thought that this particular judgment was one I should have made. He was totally unrepentant. "Christmas," he said, "is a ways off. An extra Christmas never hurt anybody." Since he supports this theory by keeping a lighted Christmas tree in front of his Palm Springs home the year round, I saw little to gain from continuing the discussion.

And then, of course, there was Beau Brummel and Quiz. Beau, a yellow Labrador, arrived at our house twenty-three Christmas Eves ago with a red bow around his neck. Ten weeks old, he was a first cousin of Frank's dog, Charlie, whom I not-so-secretly coveted. Everyone in our house loved Beau. When, fifteen years later, he had to be put to sleep, our grief was deep. After several months Frank said, "I'm going to get you another dog. It'll help. It's time, Armando." (Nicknames are a way of life with Frank. Marvin Davis, the oil and film billionaire, is "Three B"; Charlie Miller, his longtime piano player, possessor of an extraordinarily pale complexion, is "Suntan Charlie"; Yul Brynner is "the Chinaman." My all-time favorite remains "the Bookmaker," his affectionate soubriquet for the late Random House publisher, Bennett Cerf.)

I told him sharply not to surprise us, that we didn't want another dog. From time to time he would mention it. Months later, at his Palm Springs home, Frank pointed to Miss Wiggles, Barbara's King Charles spaniel. "A little dog like that, Armando, not like Beau." I said I'd think about it.

A few days later numerous photographs of tiny Kilspindie Quizzical arrived from his breeder in Maine, together with his impeccable pedigree and a long letter extolling his virtues. Quiz himself was not far behind, having made the transcontinental trip in Barbara's lap aboard the Sinatra jet. Frank and Barbara came along a few days later to admire him, signing our guest book "Aunt Barbara and Uncle Frank." Of course, Frank was right. Having another dog helped a lot.

The seat-belt sign flashes, the plane lands, and we glide to a halt. Again the limousines have formed up, and we are quickly on the move. This time a police escort leads us on our way.

As we pull to a stop at the arena's stage door, Frank is out of the car and inside the building in an instant, barely glimpsed by the people behind the barricades.

His dressing room features a lavish hors d'oeuvre table and a fully stocked bar. As Barbara urges us to dig in, Frank is briefed on who is outside. Few will make it into the inner sanctum. More often than not, particularly in a university town, they include children of his friends. Invariably they get in first. This is a high point for Frank, who has usually known them all their lives. His face lights up. "How are you?" "You working hard?" "You got the tickets? Are they okay?" "I had dinner with your mom and dad the other night. They're fine." "Come see me in New York. I'll be around awhile."

Next comes the inevitable celebrity athlete, the Mayor, and one or two others. That's it; time has run out.

As Sinatra vanishes to change into his working clothes— dinner jacket, shirt with black tie, and trousers—my mind goes back to a dressing room in Las Vegas many years ago. His piano player, Charlie Miller, had recently suffered two broken legs during one of California's dreadful mudslides, an accident that claimed Mrs. Miller's life.

Suddenly realizing that "Suntan" would not be playing with him, I asked Sinatra who would be. He told me that Count Basie was filling in. "A pretty good substitute," I noted. He agreed, but ruefully said that Basie was much tougher than Suntan. The two of them, it seems, had gone out drinking several nights before and stayed out until morning. At six-thirty that evening Sinatra realized that his voice might not be at its best that night. "If I miss a note or two along the way, follow along with me so that it sounds all right," he said to Basie. The Count looked him full in the eye and said, "I play the notes just the way they're written. The rest is up to you." It had made quite an impression on Sinatra. I asked him if he was angry at Basie. "No," he said, "but I'm not going out drinking with him anymore!"

We are barely seated when a ripple of applause starts from the point where we entered. It builds as Frank comes down the aisle, and by the time he enters the prizefight ring that serves as a stage, the audience is on its feet. He holds up his hand and nods several times without smiling. It is clearly a gesture that says, "Let's not get carried away with what's past. We're all here for tonight."

He starts easily. "I've Got the World on a String" is a typical opening. He will perform steadily for about an hour and fifteen minutes. His performance appears effortless, but Sinatra rehearses daily.

He will sing some twenty songs, many of them familiar to the audience. He always, however, includes several new songs, knowing that a few will take hold and finally become favorites.

Invariably someone will call for a favorite that has not yet been heard, and invariably he will respond chattily, "I can't keep singing the same songs. I'd get bored." This casual remark cuts deep with Frank. In 1971 boredom caught up with Sinatra, and he announced his retirement. "I've had it," he told me. "Enough's enough."

Over the next few years he learned what boredom really is, and on September 30th, 1973, he came out of retirement at the Dorothy Chandler Pavilion, for the benefit of the Los Angeles Music and Art School. It is no coincidence that both his "final" performance and his comeback were benefits. He plays ten or twelve each year, and they are most meaningful to him. A typical example is the October 30th, 1981, benefit he played at the Beverly Hilton Hotel for St. John's Hospital and Health Center in Santa Monica, California. The institution had never raised more than $150,000 for a single event. He met with the committee and told them he wanted the ballroom scaled to net them one million dollars. They were, to put it mildly, apprehensive. He sang, as he always does, without fee (many performers get paid for benefits). He obtained the services of Bob Newhart and the Fifth Dimension, paid for the orchestra and rehearsal time, and arranged for individual gifts from him at each table. He bought the first table, and a few days before the event the room was sold out. St. John's benefited to the tune of $1,300,000.

The audiences' favorites are not always Frank's own. "Strangers in the Night" is an example. Whenever he starts that song, there is applause, and he'll say tolerantly, "You still like it?" shake his head in mild disbelief, and sing on. Privately he'll say that he never liked it, but generally adds that "it has helped keep me in pizza for a long time."

A repertoire favorite is Cole Porter's "I Get a Kick Out of You." When he sings "Mere alcohol doesn't thrill me at all," he often grins or chuckles sardonically. Certainly this particular lyric is not autobiographical.

Since his marriage to Barbara eighteen years ago, he has cut down markedly on his drinking. Her sunny nature and their pleasant life together have also helped him overcome the insomnia that resulted naturally from many years of late night-club shows and, in the early days, band touring. None of this is to say, however, that he has become the average nine-to-five fellow who has a drink or two before dinner and turns in before eleven.

Literally millions of words have been written about his singing, but the magical quality that has kept him on top for over four decades defies explanation, at least by him. When I asked him about it once, he just said, "I'm damned if I know. If I did, I'd bottle it and sell it. It would be easier than singing."

He pauses only briefly between songs, responding to the applause by saying, "Thank you. Pretty song," and naming the composer, lyricist, and arranger.

After some ten songs, he calls a halt to talk to the audience for about ten minutes. He is a sports buff and whenever possible will discuss the local team. He tells a joke or two and often comments on a national or world event. These references are highly partisan; he makes no secret of his views. In Buffalo that night O. J. Simpson, the great running back, was booed because he had expressed a desire to leave and play for the Los Angeles Rams. "You people should understand that," Sinatra said sternly. "He's great. He just wants to finish his career at home. That's not so awful." A nod to the conductor, and the second part of his act gets under way.

Midway through the second half he sits back on a stool, lights a cigarette, and announces that, as the last of the saloon singers, he will sing a song about "a guy whose chick has split and left him in no mood to go out among us." It is my favorite: "One for My Baby (and One More for the Road)." Memories take over. Almost everyone in the house has been consoled somewhere along the line by a Sinatra torch song.

Every singer strives to find a great finishing song. Currently, Frank's finale is "New York, New York," and even as the music starts the audience is applauding.

We do not get to share this moment; ushers tap us on the shoulder and lead us out. As the song concludes and the standing ovation fills the building, we rush into the limousines. Frank, coming down the aisle fast, is not far behind. He jumps into the front car, and the caravan moves out, sirens wailing. We are airborne before the audience has gotten out of the parking lot.

The ride home seems short. We are all naturally exhilarated—all, that is, except Frank. Sipping a drink, still in his dinner jacket, he is simply a man coming home from work. His method of returning from the workplace by jet is, to put it mildly, unusual, but decades of doing it has made it routine to him.

Invariably someone will compliment him on his performance. He looks momentarily blank and then says briefly, "Yeah. Nice audience." The truth is that he has all but forgotten it.

As we get into the cars, he tells us that we will be having dinner at an Italian restaurant. When we arrive at the stroke of midnight, the door is held open for us by the smiling proprietor. Outnumbered by waiters and captains, we head for our special table. Barbara, list in hand, seats us. Drink orders are taken. Bottles of excellent red and white wines appear. Frank, as always, has ordered ahead, and a wide variety of tempting antipasti are soon served, followed by several pastas and a Lucullian veal Milanese sliced very thin. The Sinatras are gracious hosts, and Frank, although a light eater himself, is a lavish provider.

Italian restaurateurs regard a Sinatra visit as a higher award than the Medal of Freedom. In addition to the overwhelming desire to please him, the knowledge that their efforts will not be judged by a novice may act as a spur.

By the time we finish it is almost two-thirty; the evening has clearly drawn to an end. As we stroll out of the darkened restaurant onto the sidewalk, the limousines stand ready to take us home. It is difficult to express one's thanks. Frank recognizes this and takes the initiative. He kisses the wives and hugs the men or shakes their hands. "Good night," he says. "It was fun. Sleep well. We'll talk tomorrow. See you soon."

He has literally been out of the city less than five hours. He has entertained some fifteen thousand people memorably. He has earned a sum well into six figures. Another tiny brushstroke has been added to the vast canvas of his career.

He and Barbara get into their car and are gone.

# ME

## *and*

# JIMMY STEWART

TEN YEARS AGO Harriet and I faced a Christmas dinner alone. No children or grandchildren available to have dinner with us. No invitations from friends. It was a bleak prospect. I was complaining one night at a dinner party about our newly inherited waif role or, as Harriet put it, engaging in a Lonely Heart fishing expedition for an invitation. Jimmy Stewart's wife, Gloria, took the bait. "Come over," she said in her usual casual way, "and have Christmas dinner with us." As I was to learn, I had landed a big one and I never let go. We have been there every year since and it is a high point.

We know the Stewarts and their home very well indeed. I did not think too much about it that first Christmas night until the moment when we entered the front door. From that time on I realized we were in on something quite special. Christmas is the ideal day to demonstrate that Jimmy represents what we would all like to think of as the best in ourselves. This is pinpointed by the fact that an enormous number of Americans have spent part of their Christmas watching Jimmy in *It's a Wonderful Life*. Jimmy looks at it every year. His fan mail each year is enormous. Especially prized is a letter from a man who was depressed and discouraged at the holiday season and who had contemplated suicide until he saw the film. When asked about the film Jimmy says, "You know, this picture was not a hit when it came out. It just grew and grew and became this Christmas picture. I can't believe it." It is a typical Stewart explanation of everything that has marked his unique career. He "doesn't believe it." He "cannot understand it" or he "was lucky to be there at the right time." Nothing, of course, is that simple. The plain fact is that Jimmy is not Batman or Superman. We relate to him; he is Everyman and Christmas captures that fact.

There is always a beautiful tree decorated by Gloria and Jimmy. One of their twin daughters lives in San Francisco and the other in London, but at least one is with her parents every year. Some twenty friends are present, a few of them with their own children whom the Stewarts have known all their lives. The living room and the library are warm and inviting. The dinner itself is superb. It basically consists of the traditional fare. Somehow it seems to suggest Jimmy's small-town background, which he brought with him to Hollywood so long ago. There are a few marked differences, all underplayed. Almost every year someone has unostentatiously left a gift for Jimmy at the front door. One year, for example, it was an excellent portrait from an admirer which hangs today in the Stewart home.

Jimmy was a late bloomer at the marriage altar, marrying Gloria in 1949 when he was forty-one. He chose well—marvelously well. Gloria manages Jimmy's life, a salty, down-to-earth lady with a raucous, infectious laugh. For the past years she has handled Jimmy's frailty in a totally seamless fashion. They spend a great deal of happy time together at their home. She is a devout, gifted gardener. She is definitely not one of the local "lunch bunch." At times she protects him. At times she pushes him. When there is something that she particularly likes to do, much of his frailty seems to vanish. Northern Africa is her favorite place on earth. Hunting is anathema to her. She is an active participant in the African Wildlife Foundation. There is something that touches her basically about the terrain and the people. The friendships she has acquired are meaningful to her. Jimmy accompanies her on every trip. Each day he participates as much or as little as he chooses.

To Jimmy, Gloria can do no wrong. She will walk into a room and he will say, "You look beautiful tonight. What a wonderful dress." Gloria will respond, "Jimmy, I've worn it ten times." Jimmy repeats, "You look beautiful." She can come in from the garden in a T-shirt and jeans and he will say, "You look better than anyone I've ever seen." When they give friends vegetables from their garden he says, "These are the best vegetables in town. Gloria grew them." There is very little difference between what he has so often projected on the screen and what he projects in his daily life.

At one time during his bachelor days Jimmy shared a house with Henry Fonda, a friend from Princeton days. Jimmy is a staunch conservative; Fonda was a liberal. I have asked him how this close friendship survived for so many years without being beset by political disagreements. Jimmy's answer is brief and to the point. "We just didn't talk about that stuff," he says. "We agreed that we disagreed and left it at that." There is no incentive to press further to find out if there were particular moments of stress. He will simply repeat that it never came up. It is one of the keys to his personality. He remembers clearly the gut issue that enabled the friendship to flourish. The details do not particularly matter to him and are probably long forgotten. One element that must have made it simpler is that there had to be long periods of time where nothing was said at all. Henry was as laconic as Jimmy.

Stewart and Fonda could not have been members of a Lonely Hearts club. They were both handsome, attractive, genuine movie stars. The doorbell must have been ringing constantly. The rumor and gossip about this abound today. Once, overcome by curiosity, I tentatively questioned him about it. His answer was simple and to the point. "There's always been a lot of girls around this town," said Hollywood's great fountain of information. Oddly enough, over thirty years went by before they made *The Cheyenne Social Club*, their only film together. They both made better pictures during their careers, but they teamed wonderfully. The film deserved more kudos than it received.

Jimmy entered Princeton with a definite goal in mind. He was an engineering major. He did very poorly indeed which, in the last analysis, was the only break his acting career ever needed. By chance he became a member of the famous Princeton Triangle Club. Over a three-year period he played a variety of parts. In his senior year Joshua Logan, destined to become a famous director, saw enough merit in Jimmy to ask him to come up to Falmouth, Massachusetts, to be a part of his summer stock company. "That he happened to see me," says Stewart, "is just a good break." Good fortune seemed to dog him. Enough people saw him at Falmouth to launch his brief Broadway career. Through great good luck, he was seen by the head of Metro-Goldwyn-Mayer's casting department. Almost immediately he was given a contract at that studio. He played some small parts, but only for a brief period of time. Quickly the studio executives and the public saw something they liked. "Honesty," says George Burns, the great philosopher of show business, "is the most important thing about acting. If you can fake that you've got it made." Jimmy never had to fake it. He had it and projected it, a rarity indeed. Most film stars are manufactured, fitting and proper for the make-believe world in which they function. If Cary Grant invented himself, Jimmy had no alternative but to follow the opposite course. What he projected on film was in essence his Midwestern, middle-class background. To that he only had to add one ingredient, a gifted, well-disciplined talent. It was this mix that created Jimmy Stewart, enduring film star.

Prior to 1939 he had already appeared in some fine films such as *You Can't Take It With You*. In that vintage year, however, he starred in *Mr. Smith Goes to Washington*. He never looked back. The famous drawl quickly became his endlessly imitated trademark. There is no nightclub comedian that cannot do a ten-minute imitation of Jimmy Stewart. "Sometimes," he says, "I feel I'm imitating myself." He claims that his hesitant delivery stems from the fact that he was not a fast study. Sometimes he had to grope for the next line. That was not the fact, however, when a different technique was required. There was no stammering in the famous Hitchcock pictures such as *Rear Window* and *Vertigo*. In the Westerns, which marked the latter part of his career, the dialogue was swift and certain. The public tends to forget the tremendous intensity that Stewart brought to these films and the violence that the country boy was capable of portraying when called upon.

*Harvey*, which he did on the stage as well as on the screen, is to my mind his most unique performance. It is impossible to think of another actor, accompanied from start to finish by a six-foot rabbit invisible to everyone but him, who could make it work. Henry Koster, *Harvey*'s brilliant director, did not think that a script of *Harvey* would do it justice. He telephoned Jimmy and tried to explain the complex series of misadventures that Harvey and his owner would experience. As Koster got deeper into it, it became increasingly more convoluted. Finally he said, "I know this all sounds pretty terrible, but—" Jimmy cut him off quickly. "Henry," he said, "if you want me to play a guy who goes through life with this rabbit that is seen only by him, don't think about it twice. I'll do it." Jimmy always reacted that directly to great directors such as Frank Capra, John Ford, and Alfred Hitchcock. His instincts were very sure.

He won his first Academy Award Oscar in *The Philadelphia Story* in 1940. His father telephoned him the next day saying, "I hear you won something. What was it?" "It was a statue," his son explained. "Well," his father said, "send it along to me. I'll put it in the window of the hardware store." It resided there for many years.

Jimmy's transition from film star to military service was undoubtedly a difficult one. He had been an accomplished licensed pilot for fifteen years before he entered the Army, so flying represented no problem. The fact that he was a major film star created an initial attitude toward him that did not make his life easy. He had to convince the others that he was not someone apart, and he did it. Jim Murray, a splendid *Los Angeles Times* columnist, wrote of Jimmy Stewart's war years: "Movie actors did not have to go to war. He did. They sold bonds to build bombers. He flew the bombers. They flew over USO camp shows. He flew over Schweinfurt. They supported the war effort. He was the war effort. When he was made a Major General it was in effect a battlefield commission." Jimmy remained a member of the reserve for many decades. He retired as a Major General. Although others made much of it, Jimmy has always characteristically underplayed it.

It is difficult to think of Jimmy as an activist who would have a large hand in changing, and indeed in bringing down, the star system at the major studios. However, he did just that. At the end of the war he returned to Hollywood. His MGM contract, by coincidence, had expired. He was a free man. Both MGM and Jimmy must have thought he would re-sign. It was the custom of the day. All the big stars were under contract to one studio or another. The studios would not negotiate their basic tenet that stars could not have a share in the earnings of the films. It was enough that they were getting large, and in some cases huge, salaries. One of Jimmy's closest friends, William Goetz, who later was to be my officemate for a decade, was at that moment in time head of Universal Studios. He told Jimmy that it was out of the question for him to meet MGM's salary, but offered him a piece of the profits of his starring films. Jimmy finally elected to do just that. Three films were involved. The first two were losers, but the third, a Western, *Winchester 73*, was a smash hit. Jimmy made more money from that picture than he had over his whole career. The major studios refused to bend and the great exodus began. One after another, as their contracts ran out, the stars poured forth into the open market. It was the end of the studios' contract star system, and their leader out of the plush wilderness into the plushier wilderness was a man who never in his life thought of himself as a trailblazer.

Jimmy lives his life in a quiet but constant glow of public affection and love. It is the flip side of, for example, Madonna. Her life is lived in the constant glare of superfandom. Her performances and her recordings are high-powered happenings. Jimmy, after fifty years of public acceptance and affection, is not a hit, he is an institution. The evidences of it are all around him.

Tour buses make the rounds of homes of film and television stars on a daily basis. For the most part, the drivers pull up with the announcement of whose home is being viewed. What the tourist sees is high walls, high trees, locked gates, and an occasional security guard. The owners, not without reason, want to distance themselves as far as possible from these activities. Inaccuracies are inevitable. Much of the information being microphoned to the tourists is out-of-date.

The Stewart home is a glowing exception, a gem of authenticity. The Stewarts have lived there for forty years. There it stands, visible to the naked eye. No shielding walls, gates, or trees. Anyone is free to get out of a bus or a car and take a photograph. There is really nothing to stop them from crossing the sidewalk, walking up to the house, and ringing the doorbell. They simply do not ever do it. Their respect for Jimmy is too great.

There is sometimes an unexpected dividend. Jimmy will

come out of the house to go for a walk or to get his car, a twelve-year-old Volvo station wagon, unique in a town where cars are a status symbol. If this happens he will wave to the tour, stand quietly for a minute or two for photographs and, unmolested, go on his way. It is the way people react to this particular icon. The same individuals who would try desperately to touch Sylvester Stallone are more than satisfied to just look at Jimmy. In recounting their tour when they get home one can be certain that this is the high point of their trip.

Jimmy's promises are kept. A few years ago his agent, the late Herman Citron, came to him with the news that a publisher had offered a seven-figure advance for his autobiography. Jimmy responded that he wished it had happened several weeks ago. Recently, he explained, riding on a plane from New York to Los Angeles, his seatmate told him he was from the Public Broadcasting System. He said that if Jimmy would agree to do a program based on highlights from his films and his background it would be an enormous contribution. Jimmy finally agreed. He told Citron that he did not think there would be room for this comprehensive television work plus an autobiography. Citron was used to Jimmy's unbending point of view, almost always accepting the initial decision as final. This time, however, he mounted strong arguments based upon the value of the money as opposed to the value of the public service. "Jimmy," he said, "you have contributed your time and your talent unceasingly to charitable causes. There are many other things that you can do for the Public Broadcasting System. We're talking about money here. Big money. The mere fact that a man said something to you on a plane is not a formal contract. There's a thousand ways to get out of that. I can simply tell him that you forgot that you were committed to do a book and would not be permitted to do a comprehensive TV program." Jimmy responded that this was not the case. "I told him I would do it," he said. "If he calls I'm going through with it."

The program, hosted by Johnny Carson, who appeared in it throughout, was an outstanding television event. It took a fair amount of time from Carson's busy schedule. I asked him why he did it and he said simply, "It's Jimmy. There's only one. I wanted to do it." As so often happens, Jimmy's instincts about the book were right. He would certainly have been too modest to tell his story in a way that pleased his publisher.

Honesty certainly turned out to be its own reward. Subsequently four poems Jimmy had previously written were published in a thirty-three-page book. It made the *New York Times* Best Seller List with ease, remaining on it for many weeks. One would be hard pressed to find anyone else who could match that accomplishment.

The Stewarts are among a closely knit group of friends with whom they are completely at home. He is stoic about the fact that no hearing aid has been very successful for him. He accepts the fact that even a moderately high noise level at a small dinner tends to make him more of an onlooker of the proceedings than a participant. If there is a piano in the room and he is asked even once he will accompany himself in his rendition of "Ragtime Cowboy Joe." Knowing the words by heart, we sometimes join in the last half of the chorus. Despite the fact that he does it quite badly, it is invariably a source of considerable enjoyment to all. Familiarity does not in this case breed contempt.

No life is free from tragedy. Jimmy and Gloria are no exception. In the last days of the Vietnam war they lost a son. It was a comfort to them that they had visited the area quite recently and seen him, but it actually softened the blow very little. Perhaps his military background should have made the inevitability of such tragedies not unexpected. It did not work that way. Gloria, more ebullient than Jimmy, adjusted over time better than he did. The loss remains with him always, though it goes unspoken.

Millions of people would love to have Christmas dinner with the Stewarts, but I want them to know that I will not be pried loose from my place without putting up a struggle. If one is eager to leave the ranks of the waifs, it is ideal to start at the top.

# ME
## *and*
# A FEW THOUGHTS

As I WRITE these words I am seventy-seven years old. No matter where I happen to be when this topic comes up, people invariably say to me, "Why, that's not old at all today." I cannot bring myself to believe that. As long as I can remember, there have been only three age classifications—young, middle-aged, and old. Since I do not see many people of a hundred and fifty-four wandering around, I cannot delude myself, hard as I try, that I belong in the middle-aged group, so it is only natural that I look back a bit, which is what I have done in this book. It has been wonderful to share experiences and friendships with the people I have written about and I look forward to many great times in the years ahead.

A reader might be excused for thinking that for me it has all been ham and jam. That, of course, is not true for anybody. I have had my share of problems. I am reminded, however, of a time many years ago when I attended a gala Hollywood premiere with Sylvia and Danny Kaye for a film starring Danny. There were klieg lights, plush red restraining ropes, and shouting, screaming fans. When we were finally seated, Sylvia said to me, "Anyone looking at that scene would envy me my life. Little do they know of the problems that I have." She did indeed at that moment have a variety of problems. I responded in all candor, "The truth of the matter, Sylvia, is that if you told your problems to any of those people they would say, 'Let me have your problems and you can take mine!' " Using that standard, I do not anticipate that my problems deserve or will receive a large measure of sympathy. However, if I were given a chance to live my life over, and no one has offered me that opportunity, I like to think that I would have worked much harder. I have never been what we used to call a playboy, but I regret that I did not give more complete dedication to the work opportunities that came my way so easily. I have come to realize too late that hard work that one enjoys is the ultimate satisfaction.

I believe everyone should have a fantasy and that it is for the best if that fantasy is never realized. Answered fantasies may well possess the same perils as answered prayers. My own fantasy is to stride up the eighteenth fairway at the Masters Golf Tournament to the roar of the crowd, with an Arnold Palmer smile and wave, needing only a six-inch putt to win the title. Since I have never broken eighty, my fantasy is secure.

There have been a few people in my life whom I know and wish I had known better. Alistair Cooke's name pops at random into my mind. So does the late Norman Cousins, General Colin Powell, golf champion Raymond Floyd, and Jerusalem's Mayor Teddy Kollek. There is, of course, a short list of individuals that I know well enough to last me a lifetime.

The format of my book did not permit me to do a chapter on my wife, Harriet. My feelings for her and for our relationship would have changed the character of the book. I love her totally and cannot conceive of what my life would have been without her. I am blessed with wonderful children and grandchildren and, although many of them are geographically more removed from me than I would like, they are a source of deep, continuing pleasure. Perhaps I can write another book on that subject. I would like to try it before I am a hundred and fifty-four and have settled snugly into the old-age group.